THE MURRAY'S CHEESE HANDBOOK

THE MURRAY'S CHEESE HANDBOOK

MORE THAN 300 OF THE WORLD'S BEST CHEESES

ROB KAUFELT
and LIZ THORPE

BROADWAY BOOKS | NEW YORK

PRINTED IN THE UNITED STATES OF AMERICA

BROADWAY BOOKS and its logo, a letter B bisected on the diagonal, are trademarks of Random House, Inc.

Visit our Web site at www.broadwaybooks.com

Illustrated by Andrew Barthelmes

Library of Congress Cataloging-in-Publication Data
Kaufelt, Rob, 1947–
    The Murray's cheese handbook : more than 300 of the world's best cheeses / Rob Kaufelt with Liz Thorpe
        p.   cm.
    Includes index.
    1. Cheese. 2. Cheese—Varieties. 3. Cookery (Cheese) I. Thorpe, Liz, 1978– II. Title.

    SF271.K38 2006
    641.3'73—dc22

                                        2006043945

ISBN-13: 978-0-7679-2130-5
ISBN-10: 0-7679-2130-5

10 9 8 7 6 5 4 3 2 1

First Edition

This book is dedicated to my parents,
Florence and Stanley Kaufelt,
who kept the faith
despite all the early evidence.

CONTENTS

Acknowledgments

The cheese road is long and winding, and I wish to thank several people who have helped along the way:

My collaborator and colleague, Liz Thorpe, is among the best and the brightest of the next generation in cheese. The staff at Murray's have been fantastic, especially those who have been with me for so long: Frankie Meilak, my right-hand man; Vicki Potaznik, who kept me from going broke; Cielo Peralta, the greatest counterman of all time; Krish Madhavan, who goes back to the beginning.

Thanks to the cheesemongers and *affineurs* at home and abroad, especially Steve Jenkins, Joe Moscowitz, Gerd Stern, Randolph Hodgson, Seamus Sheridan, Will Studd, Enric Canut, and especially Hervé Mons.

Special thanks to Tamasin Day-Lewis, who travels the earth with me, exploring its wondrous delights.

And finally, a fond farewell to Bridget Watkins, whom Jenkins and I would visit back in the old days when the American Cheese Society was young and headquartered around the corner on Downing Street, and who made us laugh, and whose passing has left us with less light but a brighter angel.

Rob Kaufelt
Greenwich Village

For my part, thanks to Rob Kaufelt for taking on a wide-eyed kid who thought cheese was neat some four years ago.

Adrian Murcia, for endless help, enthusiasm, and support in the delights of wine, beer, and cheese; Sasha Davies, whose passion makes work a pleasure each day; Clelia Peters, my rock; and above all, my brilliant mother, for never thinking I was crazy to start this cheese gig in the first place, or not saying so if she did.

Liz Thorpe
Brooklyn

INTRODUCTION

I've always loved cheese, but I didn't become passionate about it until I became a customer at Murray's myself back in 1989. If I think back to my earliest cheese memories, they are not about eating the perfect Piave in Italy. They are about growing up eating cheeseburgers and grilled cheese sandwiches in Highland Park, New Jersey, and about Mom cooking Dad those big, puffy, brown cheese omelets on a Sunday with Swiss or Cheddar

Almost everybody loves cheese and has some favorites. The magic is that you can go on discovering cheese almost forever; there are thousands of different cheeses from all over the world. The most amazing thing about them all is that the three main ingredients remain the same—milk, rennet, and salt—and yet the tastes, textures, and appearance are infinite in their variety. It's amazing, too, that cheese has been made the same way continuously for thousands of years.

I don't think my love of cheese is distinguishable from the idea of buying something uniquely delicious and perfectly ripened from an old shop in an old neighborhood, and that's the experience I want all my customers to have in the new Murray's.

When I first became a customer at the old Murray's, one of the things I liked best about it, and still do, is that it is the oldest cheese shop in New York. As I write this, in October 2005, Murray's is celebrating its sixty-fifth anniversary. It may have moved three times, but it's traveled only twenty-five feet from the original shop in all that time.

I never met the original owner, Murray Greenberg; he died before I got here. He was an Eastern European Spanish Civil War veteran, and when he came to America in 1940 he opened a wholesale butter and egg shop a few doors up Cornelia Street. Despite his communist leanings, I've been told he was a street-smart capitalist who used to buy cheese cheap, trim it up, and sell it.

In the 1970s, he finally sold the shop to his clerk, Louis Tudda, an Italian immigrant from Calabria, who filled the shop not just with cheese but also with cheap olive oil and tomatoes, which he sold mostly to his local Italian neighbors. That's the way it was when I bought the shop fifteen years ago in 1991. So what made me buy it and give up everything for cheese? I had left the family supermarket business in 1985 to work in full-service specialty shops in New Jersey, where I was from. When my second shop in Princeton tanked with the crash of '87, I found myself in my brother's place here in the Village, wondering what I should do with my life next.

One day I was standing in line at the original Murray's, and I heard Louis say he'd lost his lease and was closing. I made him several offers he refused, but eventually made a deal. I moved the shop to the corner of Bleecker, and that's where it remained for fourteen years, until November 2004.

Frankie Meilak, who had worked for Louis for six years, came with the shop. He is still here with me. He lived up the street and stayed on when his parents moved back home to Malta. Louis stayed on for a year before he went back home.

One day around ten years ago, Cielo Peralta walked into the shop and announced he was coming to work for me. I told him I didn't have a job for him. He took absolutely no notice, strode right past me straight into the shop, put on an apron, and started selling cheese, saying I didn't have to pay him unless I liked his work. I only had to see Cielo behind the counter for a day to know he'd sell twelve times more cheese than anyone else. In fact, he's probably sold more specialty cheese than anyone else in the United States. He's still here, too.

When I arrived at Murray's we were selling around 100 different cheeses. We've gone from 100 to 250 on the counter at any one time, but with our seasonal calendar and promotions, our range is probably somewhere around 500 to 600 cheeses.

We started broadening our selection in the early nineties, a time of explosive interest in U.S. and foreign artisanal food. Our original American purveyors (pioneer women) had started making cheese—like Mary Keehn's Humboldt Fog and Cindy Major's Vermont Shepherd—in the seventies and eighties. There were cheeses from places with no tradition of cheesemaking, or where the tradition had been nearly lost and where it began anew. I got involved in American farmstead cheeses first through the American Cheese Society, whose headquarters in those days were around the corner from the shop on Downing Street.

I think the first real specialty cheese we got from abroad came from Neal's Yard Dairy in England in the early 1990s. After that, I went to Spain, Italy, France, Ireland, and England searching out small dairies and new cheeses, but I still thought the growing popularity and appetite for cheese was probably a fad; I didn't know it was going to turn into a lasting trend.

My father thought buying Murray's was a really stupid idea. We were at the peak of the low-fat, cholesterol-obsessed days, and there was clearly no expectation from him, as an experienced grocer, or from me, that cheese was going to become the Next Big Thing. It's only in the last couple of years that artisanal cheese has penetrated the consciousness of a broader market in the U.S.

In the beginning, I got into cheese because I wanted a nice little old-fashioned business like the one in the picture hanging over my dairy case. It shows my grandfather's shop in Perth Amboy, New Jersey, in 1925. My grandfather Irving with his wife, Fanny, and his brother Murray with his wife, Bessie, and their two small children, are all sitting on the stoop in front. Buying Murray's was a romantic notion. There had always been a line when I went there as a customer, so I thought it was conceivable that I could lead a Greenwich Village life, pay the rent and buy groceries, and take my place in that long family tradition. I also liked the fact we're on Bleecker Street, because I grew up listening to Bob Dylan and Dave Van Ronk. Van Ronk turned out to be a Murray's customer and gave me guitar lessons before he died.

I like the idea of being a small business and of buying from small businesses. The cheesemakers I deal with love what they're doing, are passionate about making cheese, and are peculiar, quirky oddballs, like I am. I also don't have to wear a suit and tie!

I love the creative aspect of merchandising food. I believe coming to Murray's should be an entertaining experience; it's fun, it's funky, it's exciting. My favorite food-buying experiences have been in the markets in European villages and towns, where everything is simple and direct. The food is abundantly on display, and you often buy from the producer directly. The transaction has a theatrical element to it: The sellers are onstage and you, the customer, are the audience.

One of the things I always liked best about Murray's was that the people behind the counter would explain cheese to the customers without making them feel like they were idiots. The truth is, if we educate the customers, suggest new things, tempt them with ever more delicious cheeses, and let them taste things over the counter, they'll enjoy cheese even more and buy more of it. That may be one of the oldest traditions in retail, but it's the one that's nearly been killed in our chain-store age.

So I wrote this book to tell you all about cheese, to pass on my passion.

Here are my favorite three hundred or so cheeses out of the thousands I've tasted. I hope you will sit down with a glass of wine, a hunk of good cheese, and this book, and savor all three. This guide is designed so you can easily consult it, dipping into various sections for useful and practical information. And when you're in the neighborhood, stop by Murray's and let us look after you. Cheese is my job and my passion, and what more can I say about my work than that, fifteen years later, I still can't wait to taste another new cheese.

HOW to Use THIS HANDBOOK

Each cheese is followed by a quick and simple overview of its key characteristics: milk type, country of origin, raw versus pasteurized, type, vegetarian, and controlled designation of origin.

MILK TYPE

First off, we'll tell you if a cheese is:

Water buffalo
Cow
Goat
Sheep
Mixed (and which blend)

Most commonly seen are cheeses made from goat's, cow's, and sheep's milk. Some cheeses are made from water buffalo milk. Others are a mixture of two or more milk types. The type of milk affects the flavor, texture, and character of a cheese. It's difficult to make generalizations, but we comfortably claim the following.

Goat's milk has less fat and tends to taste lighter and fresher. Also, it's often made into lightly aged styles that have a fresh, tangy taste.

Cows make the most milk, and you'll see the greatest variety of type, texture, and flavor in cow's-milk cheeses. They account for the majority of cheese (just check out the index by milk type).

Sheep have the fattiest milk, which translates into rich, hearty cheese, even if it's aged and drier in texture. You feel the fat.

Buffalo, goat, and sheep milk are most likely to have "barny" or "gamy" flavors, like rare meat.

COUNTRY OF ORIGIN

Maybe you're a Francophile, or planning to visit the Basque country. Perhaps you have a passion for all things Italian, or you've got a recipe that calls for something Swiss. Knowing where a cheese originates may not guarantee a specific eating experience, but it's always a good idea to have that information.

Specific types of cheese are often typical of certain regions. That's no surprise if you consider that the climate and types of animals raised are consistent within a given area. Our descriptions will always point you to the region of production.

RAW VERSUS PASTEURIZED

Cheese may be made from milk that is either raw or pasteurized; some cheeses are available in both raw and pasteurized versions. Things to note:

- In the United States, all cheese that is less than sixty days old must, by law, be made from pasteurized milk. This is true for both imported and domestically produced cheese. Under sixty days=pasteurized.

- In the United States, doctors typically recommend that pregnant women avoid raw milk cheese, though this is not necessarily the case in Europe.

- We find that pasteurization often results in a cheese that has less flavor and a gummier texture. That said, many pasteurized cheeses, such as Stilton, have superb flavor.

For more on raw milk and pasteurization (and what we *really* think), see Frequently Asked Questions.

Different books break down cheeses into various types, styles, or families. We have divided our handbook into seven types that we find clear and simple to understand:

Fresh
Bloomy
Washed Rind
Semisoft
Firm
Hard
Blue

These types are about more than texture or cheesemaking approach. They're about a group of cheeses that provide a consistent eating experience. We're guessing the technical stuff is secondary to your interest in finding a cheese you like. Our types will help you do that.

Fresh
Think: Young. Tart. Tangy. Lemony. Smooth. Moist. Creamy. No rind.
Find: Fresh goat cheese (chèvre), mozzarella

Bloomy
Refers to the snowy, fluffy, "blooming" rind.
Think: White. Buttery. Decadent. Pillowy. Fluffy. Rich. Mild to mushroomy. Edible rind.
Find: Brie, Camembert, triple-crèmes (Brillat Savarin, Cremeux de Bourgogne)

Washed Rind
These are washed during aging in brine (salt water), beer, wine, or spirits.

Think: Pungent. Stinky. Fruity. Meaty. Intense. Aromatic. Vibrant pink to orange edible rind.

Find: Epoisses de Bourgogne, Livarot, Pont-l'Evêque, Taleggio

Semisoft

Think: Pliable. Earthy. Wet straw. Hay. Leaves. Melting.

Find: Fontina, Garrotxa, Morbier, Tomme de Savoie

Firm

Think: Dense but supple. Grassy. Eggy. Fruited. Sharp. Thick, natural rind not typically eaten.

Find: Cheddar, Gruyère, Manchego, Ossau-Iraty-Brebis Pyrénées

Hard

Think: The super-aged big guns. Dry. Crunchy. Caramelly. Butterscotchy. Grainy.

Find: Aged Gouda, Dry Jack, Parmigiano-Reggiano

Blue

Think: Mold! Veins. Craters. Big. Sharp-edged. Punchy. Complex.

Find: Gorgonzola, Roquefort, Stilton

VEGETARIAN

A cheese may be considered vegetarian if, during cheesemaking, curds were coagulated with a non-animal substance. To our knowledge, this is the first resource to identify the cheeses of the world by coagulant.

For more on this distinction, see Frequently Asked Questions.

CONTROLLED DESIGNATION OF ORIGIN

Various European countries bestow the honor "controlled designation of origin" on foodstuffs of the highest quality, often produced using traditional methods, and usually reflecting a unique environment that promotes distinctive flavor characteristics. In France, this protection is the A.O.C. (Appellation d'Origine Contrôlée). In Italy, it is the D.O.P. (Denominazione di Origine Protetta). For Portugal, it's D.O.P. (Denominação de Origem Protegida). In Spain, the term is D.O. (Denominación de Origen).

Knowing that a cheese has a controlled designation of origin won't necessarily tell you what it will taste like, but it guarantees the following:

Origin: The milk is produced and the cheese is made in a precise geographical area (e.g., the town of Meaux).

Tradition: Traditional cheesemaking methods (such as burying a cheese in the ground or producing only during certain months) may go back thousands of years and produce the unique "recipe" for that cheese.

Character: The typical characteristics of each cheese, such as shape, size, rind, texture, and minimum fat content, may be regulated.

Authenticity: The governing country guarantees authenticity and quality: Producers submit to approval by a commission.

American cheesemaking has no equivalent control at this time. Domestic farmstead cheeses are produced by single farms, rather than co-ops or groups, which means identification of the producer is essential. Thus, in this guide, all American cheeses are listed first by producer and second by cheese name.

Some of the most famous cheeses in the world do not benefit from "controlled designation of origin" protection. This, unfortunately, is why a divine raw cow's-milk wheel from a single farm in Somerset, England, *and* a plastic-wrapped slice of industrial "cheese food" from origins unknown may both be deemed "Cheddar."

We won't swear that every "controlled designation of origin" cheese will be good, but it does promote consistency, because all cheeses with the same name must subscribe to the same regulations. It also suggests that you'll be eating a unique piece of a country's culture, history, and tradition.

FREQUENTLY ASKED
QUESTIONS

In sixty-five years the Murray's staff has accumulated a fair amount of cheese knowledge. Here are answers to customers' top ten questions about cheese.

1. WHAT'S THE DIFFERENCE BETWEEN RAW AND PASTEURIZED MILK?

Raw milk is milk straight from the animal, with no treatment of any kind. It's how milk was consumed—in liquid form, as cheese, and as fermented dairy products like yogurt and sour cream—for thousands of years. Raw milk is a living substance, full of bacteria and enzymes, that, when gathered from healthy animals under sterile conditions, is naturally "in check." Beneficial, healthful bacteria prevent potentially harmful bacteria from multiplying and contaminating the milk.

Pasteurized milk is milk that has been heat treated using a method developed by nineteenth-century French scientist Louis Pasteur. Pasteurization, initially developed to prevent wine from souring, can be used to kill unwanted bacteria in many kinds of food.

There are several types of pasteurization:

1. Gentle pasteurization: Milk is heated to 145°F for thirty minutes and cooled.

2. High-temperature, short-time (HTST) pasteurization: Milk is heated to 161°F for fifteen seconds and cooled.

3. Ultra-high-temperature (UHT) pasteurization: Milk is heated to 200°F for several seconds and cooled before being packed in aseptic containers that require no refrigeration.

In the United States, pasteurization is mandatory for all cheese aged less than sixty days. This applies to domestic cheese and imported cheese. If a cheese is less than two months old, it must be pasteurized to be sold legally.

The history of pasteurized dairy in the United States begins in the late nineteenth century. Milk was a crucial food for the growing population, especially the poorer immigrant populations that were streaming into congested urban environments.

Unfortunately, milk was increasingly produced in unsanitary conditions. In crowded, dirty, and unhygienic barns, cows were fed the poisonous by-product from whiskey distilleries; refrigeration was limited; closed vats did not exist; tuberculosis and brucellosis were commonplace, and workers could easily transmit disease to exposed milk.

This "distillery milk" was readily available, and inexpensive, but it was teeming with dangerous pathogens. As a result, infant mortality was rampant. The solution to this problem was the pasteurization of milk. Pasteurized milk could be safely consumed, though its quality was inferior. Under these circumstances, pasteurization became a life-saving reform, but did nothing to address the root of the problem: sick animals, irresponsible dairying, and contaminated milk.

By 1949, pasteurization was mandated for all drinking milk, with the limited exception of "certified raw milk," available in a handful of states. Many advances have occurred, but the safety of today's modern, industrial system of milk production, which uses thousands of gallons of milk from dozens of sources, much of which is trucked for miles, remains tenuous. There are too many variables to ensure the safety of raw milk: One sick cow, too much temperature variance, and the whole batch can be contaminated. On this commercial scale, pasteurization remains a necessity.

2. IS RAW MILK CHEESE BETTER?

In a word, absolutely!

Pasteurization remains necessary on an industrial, commercial scale. But the highest-quality milk isn't produced on this scale, nor is the finest-quality cheese. If we thought raw milk cheese was unsafe, even though it tasted better, we wouldn't take the gamble. For us, the point goes back to the scale of production. A single farmer in northern Vermont who tends a herd of forty cows that graze on fresh grass; milks these animals twice each day in his clean, roomy barn and milking parlor; and pumps this fresh milk directly from cow to cheesemaking vat is producing a clean, safe, raw product. He can ensure control, sanitation, and healthy animals. This is pristine milk. And for us, it can become delicious, healthy, raw milk cheese.

Raw milk from grass-fed cows contains more vitamin A, vitamin B_6, vitamin C, omega-3 fats, and a host of beneficial enzymes and bacteria that aid digestion and build immunity. The enzymes lipase, lactase, and phosphatase (all damaged by pasteurization) are essential for the body to digest fats and lactose and to absorb the calcium in milk. There's no way around the fact that raw milk (and cheese) is healthier for you.

Pasteurization does a lot of damage to milk, and even the most conscientious cheesemaker faces challenges in overcoming this damage. The beneficial bacteria and enzymes that aid cheesemaking (and, it warrants saying, drive off pathogenic bacteria that can flourish in pasteurized milk) are seriously compromised or destroyed by pasteurization. Enzymes are responsible for the breakdown of fats and proteins in aging cheese, a breakdown that creates the flavors and aromas that determine the cheese's very character. Inhibited enzymes mean diminished flavor and stunted aroma. This is why pasteurized cheese is often considered to be blander, and generally less tasty, than raw milk cheese.

Preferring raw milk cheese isn't about sticking it to The Man or scoring some of that *wink, wink* contraband Camembert. It's about a four-thousand-year history of choosing the tastiest, most deliciously satisfying, and healthiest food possible.

3. HOW DO YOU MAKE CHEESE?

These are the basic steps in making any kind of cheese.

Milk: Procure the freshest, cleanest milk possible.

Pasteurize (optional): If milk is to be pasteurized, this occurs prior to cheesemaking. The gentlest method of pasteurization produces the most flavorful cheese.

Acidify: Perhaps you've heard the adage that cheesemaking is the "controlled spoilage of milk." Acidification is the first visible step of transforming liquid milk into solid curd. This can happen in two ways:

1. Milk can be left to acidify naturally, a process wherein bacteria in milk con-

sume lactose (sugar), producing lactic acid. Unaided acidification occurs over a relatively long period of time (twelve to twenty-four hours), under warm conditions (70°F to 115°F).

2. Starter (lactose-eating bacteria) can be added to milk to speed up the process of acidification, which may then be completed in fifteen minutes to several hours. Aside from lactic cultures, other microbial cultures may be added at this point, including spores that become the bloomy rind of Brie and ripening cultures that develop into the smear on washed-rind cheeses like Epoisses. Acidification increases the acidity of the milk and begins to denature the milk proteins (casein), causing them to clump together and trapping fats and other solids. Yogurts and other lactic (fresh) cheeses rely solely on acidification for the formation of curds.

Coagulate: Coagulant contains enzymes that complete the separation of protein and liquid, resulting in curds (solid) and whey (liquid). Coagulant may be of animal, microbial (mold or yeast), or vegetable (plant) origin. Coagulant attacks the protein structures of milk and corrodes the outer casing of protein molecules, causing them to knit together.

Stir/Cut: Stirring may begin while coagulation is still under way. Both stirring and cutting impact the acidity level (which, in turn, impacts the final flavor) and the final texture of a cheese. More stirring encourages curds to shed moisture, and less moisture means less potential acidity. The French refer to this process as "delactosing." Curds are subjected to mechanical action (cutting and stirring) until the proper moisture levels are achieved. This limits the potential for the development of acidity. Cutting of curds impacts texture in that tiny, rice-sized curds shed more liquid, resulting in harder paste (like Swiss Gruyère), while big, spongy curds with minimal handling retain liquid, resulting in softer texture (like Brie). Some cheeses (like Cheddar) are "milled," meaning the curds are run through a machine that grinds them into bits.

Cook: Not all cheeses are cooked, but the addition of this step (which may happen concurrently with stirring and cutting) releases even more liquid, resulting in a firmer texture. It also cooks sugars remaining in the milk after acidification, creating a sweeter, caramelized flavor. Not surprisingly, the harder cheeses are often cut and cooked (as in Parmigiano-Reggiano).

Drain: Draining off the liquid (whey) leaves the solid curds, which will be formed into cheese.

Mold: The curds are placed in molds, baskets, or hoops to mold them into various wheel shapes and sizes and to continue the process of draining.

Press: Pressing further extracts liquid, and may be gentle and brief (as for many semi-soft cheeses, like Tomme de Savoie) or steady and long (as for mountain cheeses like Gruyère that are pressed repeatedly for hours). Some soft cheeses are not pressed at all. Longer pressing creates a firmer final texture.

Salt: With the addition of salt, curds become cheese. Salt may be added in several ways. Curds may be salted directly, before wheels are formed, as in the case of Cheddar and Cantal; wheels may be hand salted; or wheels may be submerged in brine baths for several hours or many days. Parmigiano-Reggiano spends as long as twenty-four days in brine before maturation begins. Salt, in addition to being a preservative, stops the acidification process and marks the beginning of the aging process.

Age: The aging of a cheese is as important as cheesemaking itself. Varying conditions of temperature and humidity, coupled with treatments such as turning, brushing, or washing the wheels, determine rind development and profoundly impact final flavor and texture.

4. WHAT'S VEGETARIAN CHEESE?

During coagulation, protein solids are separated from liquid whey. Traditionally, the coagulant used was rennet. Rennet is extracted from the stomach lining of an animal that has not been weaned; it is necessary in the digestion of the mother's milk.

Because rennet is an animal product, a cheese is considered vegetarian when it has been coagulated using something else. The most common alternative is microbial rennet, which is derived from molds or yeast with a molecular structure similar to the active enzyme in rennet. Microbial rennet may be genetically modified.

Another vegetarian coagulant is cardoon thistle or artichoke, most often used in cheeses from southern Spain and Portugal. These cheeses are made of sheep's milk and have a particular piquant, vegetal flavor unlike any other.

5. WHAT ARE THE DIFFERENCES AMONG COW'S, GOAT'S, AND SHEEP'S MILK?

All milk is made of protein, fat, carbohydrates (sugar, or lactose), and water. Here's a comparison of average milk composition.

	COW	GOAT	SHEEP
FAT	4.2	3.6	7.0
PROTEIN	3.5	3.2	5.6
LACTOSE	4.9	4.7	4.7

Sheep's milk also has greater amounts of riboflavin, thiamine, niacin, pantothenic acid, vitamin B_6, folic acid, vitamin B_{12}, biotin, calcium, phosphorus, sodium, magnesium, zinc, and iron. In general, goat's milk has greater amounts of these vitamins and minerals than cow's milk, with the exception of riboflavin, folic acid, and vitamin B_{12}.

Worth noting is that goat's and sheep's milk are good alternatives for people who have difficulty drinking cow's milk. Allergies to the protein in cow's milk are common, and it is more difficult for the body to digest. Goat's and sheep's milk are naturally homogenized: The fat particles are smaller and evenly distributed throughout the milk, rather than separating into cream as they do in cow's milk. Consider the fact that sheep's and goat's milk are, in general, nutritionally richer than cow's milk, but both animals produce far less quantity, making their milk (and the cheese that's made from it) more labor-intensive and often more expensive. The exception to this is the Jersey cow, which contains more protein, minerals, vitamins, and butterfat than any other breed. The rich milk (5 to 6 percent butterfat) is nearly twice as rich as the "industry-standard" Holstein milk, which runs 3 to 3.5 percent butterfat.

6. WHAT DOES IT MEAN FOR A CHEESE TO BE "IN (OR OUT OF) SEASON"?

Like fruits and vegetables, good cheese has a season. It may be available all the time, but that doesn't mean it's equally good all year round. Some cheeses are simply unavailable for months at a time. A cheese's season relates to the kind of animal that is being milked, as well as the time of year the cheese is produced.

The question to ask yourself about cheese and seasonality is: When was this cheese made? You'll need a rough idea of how old it is, but from there you can backtrack and consider what the animals were eating, what the weather may have been like, and whether those factors are likely to create a great cheese or a mediocre one.

Goats: The breeds typically used for cheesemaking have a definite breeding season, which runs from August to December/January. During this time, female goats come into heat every twenty-one days. With a gestation time of approximately five months, it is natural for there to be a gap, or reduction in cheesemaking, for several months in late winter. Bigger, more industrial producers of goat's-milk cheese will freeze curd (see Frequently Asked Question #10 for why you should never freeze cheese) during the abundant summer months for use in the restricted winter months. Producers may also manipulate the natural reproductive cycle using hormones, which allows them to milk all year.

Since most goat cheeses are small and relatively young (two weeks to two months), you will likely be eating them in the same season they were produced. Even if milk is available in winter months, diverse and flavorful flora is not. Goats are great eaters: branches, leaves, bushes, and flowers are all on the menu. During the winter, however, their diet is far less varied. Even good hay is one-note, and the possibilities for nuanced and complex cheese are few.

Goat cheeses are at their best from April to November. The exception to this is aged cheese, which we like from December to March. The longer aging period (three to five months) means summer milk can be enjoyed in the dead-of-winter gloom.

Sheep: Sheep, too, have a definite breeding season. The easy way to remember it is to know you're looking for any month with an *r*. So: January, February, March, April, September, October, November, and December, during which time ewes come into heat every seventeen days. This natural inclination can be manipulated hormonally. As with goats, the gestation period is about five months. The style of cheese being produced has a considerable impact on seasonality. We see many aged varieties from American producers, which require three to six months of aging after production. Also, when breeding sheep, producers must consider the time of year the animals will be milking. If you're in Vermont, it's hardly desirable to breed in April. Lambs aren't born until September, and by then you're heading into winter. To maximize the lush summer grazing months, it's ideal to breed in fall and occupy the winter months with pregnant sheep.

Remember to consider the aging period, for cheeses *produced* from April to October are the finest. This may not mean you're eating them during this time. One of the classic American sheep cheeses, Major Farm Vermont Shepherd, is not available until August, and by Easter it's gone. Another favorite, Pyrénées Brebis, hits its stride in January. The combination of summer milk and a solid six months of age creates a phenomenal caramelized flavor that can't be found in the wheels we receive in July, which are either well aged (but made from winter milk) or the first wheels from spring (but only four months old).

Cows: Cows don't have a breeding season, but they do have the longest gestation period: nine months.

Again, cheeses produced from April to October tend to be the most flavorful. The depth and variety of flavor in milk fueled by high-altitude grasses, herbs, and flowers is so profound that many of France's best cheeses, such as Beaufort d'Alpage and

Salers, are restricted to summer production. It's not until December, however, that we begin to see these wheels, and in the case of Beaufort d'Alpage, we're talking about cheese from the previous summer—over one year old.

There are exceptions to this, notably the winter-only cheese Vacherin Mont d'Or. We've also found that bloomy and washed-rind cow's-milk cheeses are deliciously soft and runny in the winter due to a higher fat content in the milk.

7. ISN'T CHEESE GOING TO MAKE ME FAT AND GIVE ME HEART DISEASE?

The short answer is no, if you're eating quality cheese in moderation.

The long answer is more complicated. The points to make about cheese and good (or bad) health are these:

1. Come by Murray's and check out our employees. We're all in decent shape, and every one of us consumes far more cheese than the average American. Seriously, we taste cheese all day.

2. Human beings have been eating fat and cholesterol in the form of meat and eggs since the Stone Age, and in the form of dairy and cheese for ten thousand years. Heart disease and obesity as medical phenomena came on the scene about a hundred years ago. That's around the

same time that our food became industrialized: loaded with hydrogenated vegetable oil, sugar, corn oil, and the like. Moderation in all things is still wise advice, so you might not want to eat a pound of cheese every day; however real cheese doesn't cause disease. Processed, hydrogenated vegetable oil and orange dye in the remarkable fat-free cheese do. And they don't taste as good.

3. Processed milk (and cheese made from processed milk) likely contributes to heart disease. These processed products usually contain dried milk powder, a source of oxidized cholesterol that causes arteriosclerosis. Many low-fat and nonfat dairy products have some (if not all!) reconstituted dried milk.

4. Cheese made from the milk of grass-fed cows, which is likely to be unpasteurized, is good for you! It aids digestion, builds immunity, and helps your body process fat and absorb calcium. Go back and read why raw milk cheese is better.

5. Finally, fat in cheese is based on dry matter. Soft, rich, gooey cheeses are mainly water. Though they taste decadent, ounce for ounce you're eating less fat than if you ate hard cheese. But we're convinced that it's only a matter of time before science proves real cheese is good for you, just like red wine and olive oil.

8. DO I EAT THE RIND?

First and foremost, eat what you want. Some people don't enjoy the rind because its flavor is more concentrated or its texture provides too much of a contrast. Our general guidelines: If you're not sure, eat your cheese from the inside out. The flavors will be stronger the closer you get to the rind, and if you don't like the paste just beneath the rind, you probably won't like the rind itself. When deciding whether or not to eat the rind, we think of skins versus crusts. Skins are meant to be eaten, crusts are optional. For example:

Types of Cheese: Fresh, bloomy, washed-rind, some blues
Skin: If the rind is soft and appears to be a cohesive part of the cheese, even if it's blanketed in a downy coat of mold or covered in a thick, glistening smear of orange, go for it. For cheese like Brie or Taleggio, much of the aroma and flavor come from the mold or bacteria of the rind.

Types of Cheese: Semisoft, firm, some blues
Damp Crust: If the rind is thick, ridged, and smells like wet earth, you're less likely to enjoy it. The rinds on Tomme de Savoie or Saint-Nectaire tend to taste like their aromas: wet straw, earth, hay. They're rustic, to say the least. Also, with a thicker rind, which can feel gritty in the mouth, there will be a marked textural contrast.

Types of Cheese: Firm, hard
Dry Crust: If the rind is hard, waxed, or covered in plastic, you probably don't want to eat it. It won't hurt you, but, again, it will taste like it smells: wax and plastic. Not the best. Classics in this group are the aged cheeses like Parmigiano-Reggiano, Pecorino Toscano, Gruyère, and Manchego.

Generally, the younger a cheese, the more edible its rind, which makes good sense. The rind provides a barrier between the interior paste and the outside air. Over time, this barrier hardens, and cheesemakers often promote a sturdy barrier by brushing, oiling, rubbing, and in extreme cases, covering the cheese in a material like wax.

9. HOW DO I KNOW IF A CHEESE IS GOOD?

Visit a good cheese counter and you're likely to see lots of fur and fuzz. Orange, yellow, and blue cheese. Hard, soft, and everywhere in between. You may not like every cheese, but there's a difference between "stinky" and "overripe," or between "spicy" and "ammoniated."

Here are our guidelines by cheese type to help you separate the good from the bad.

Fresh (rindless)
Good: White, glistening, clean; milky aroma
Bad: Patches of blue or red mold; sharp or sour aroma

Fresh (rind, as in small goat cheese)
Good: Mottled black, gray, blue, or green mold on the rind; fluffy or chalky texture; hay and grass aroma
Bad: Excessively runny or oozing; strong dirty-animal aroma

Bloomy
Good: Fluffy white rind with some brown mottling; even texture like the web between your fingers; milky, mushroomy, wet-straw aroma
Bad: Wet, slimy, or cracked rind; red and brown patches; firm texture (underripe); super-runny texture and ammonia aroma (overripe)

Washed Rind
Good: Damp orange or pink rind; even texture like the web between your fingers; soupy texture if served in a wooden box; pungent (bacony, meaty, barny) aroma
Bad: Cracked, slimy rind; brown or black discoloration under the rind; white speckles on the rind (salt has crystallized on the surface); strong ammonia or decayed aroma

Semisoft, Firm, and Hard
Good: Even, consistent color of paste; nut, grain, and hay aroma
Bad: Spots of blue or green mold on cut surface; "sweat" (butterfat that has leached out of the cheese); dark discoloration around perimeter; plastic or strong ammonia aroma

Blue
Good: White to yellow paste; patches or veins of blue-gray-green mold (it's intentional!)
Bad: Brown color; mushy or slimy texture; strong ammonia aroma

10. HOW CAN I BEST STORE CHEESE AT HOME?

Our number one recommendation is to buy smaller pieces of cheese more often, because a reputable cheesemonger is better equipped to store cheese. That said, here are our guidelines for home storage.

Wrapping
Most references will tell you never, never, never wrap your cheese in plastic wrap. And with good reason. If you're like us, you buy a bunch of cheese, put it in your fridge, and forget about it for two weeks. By then, the cheese has been tightly wrapped, never seeing the light of day, never getting any fresh air, and it has died of suffocation. Seriously. Cheese is a living food. It needs to breathe. The rind on bloomy and washed-rind cheese cannot survive without oxygen. The exposed surface of Parmigiano-Reggiano will get sweaty and then dry out without fresh air.

But for most people at home, what are your choices?

We say: Be realistic. Wrap first in wax paper to protect the surface flavor of a cheese, and then in plastic wrap or foil to ensure it can't dry out. Promise not to forget about the cheese. Change its wrapping every couple of days, which also gives an excuse to nab a small bite.

Foil alone is okay for higher-moisture blue cheeses.

Storage and Aging

The vegetable drawer is slightly warmer and moister than the rest of the fridge, and so provides a less hostile environment. Plus, it prevents cross-contamination of flavors and aromas with other food in your fridge.

Special cheese cellars and refrigerators are a hot trend right now, but we've had respectable success "aging" cheese the old-fashioned way. Take a plastic storage container, line it with a damp paper towel, and poke holes in the lid for air. It's the perfect abode for a cheese that's not quite ripe.

Shelf Life

The life of a cheese depends on the type. Here is a rough guide by type:

    Fresh: 7 days
    Bloomy: 10–12 days
    Semisoft: 14 days
    Washed rind: 10–14 days
    Firm: 14–20 days
    Hard: Up to a month
    Blue: 10–14 days

If your firm or hard cheeses develop blue or green surface mold, the cheese is not lost. Simply scrape off and enjoy. That same surface mold in a store is a sign that the cheese has been sitting around for too long after being cut.

If you have a bigger piece of cheese, you may want to cut off a thin slice that was next to the foil or wax paper/plastic wrapping. We call this "facing," and it simply exposes new, fresh cheese underneath.

Old cheese won't hurt you, it just won't taste as good as it could.

ABBAYE DE CÎTEAUX

FRANCE | RAW | WASHED RIND

Burgundy, known for austere wines and stinky cheese, produces this plump patty made by the Abbey of Saint-Nicolas-lès-Cîteaux from the milk of a herd of fewer than a hundred Montbellarde cows. Washed daily in brine and roucou, a plant-derived coloring, the edible, cantaloupe-colored rind is relatively mild, with a thick, slippery, bulging interior that tastes like buttery, charcoal-grilled corn. Whereas the abbey itself has a history of nearly a thousand years, this cheese has been made only since 1925. Production runs to about sixty tons per year, but most of it stays in Burgundy. When you find it here, enjoy it with a delicate, aromatic Beaujolais.

ABONDANCE

FRANCE | RAW | FIRM | A.O.C.

A superlative production, originally made in the year 1000 by the monks of the Abondance monastery. Louis XVI gave it high marks, and the cheese was awarded A.O.C. protection in 1990. In the Haute-Savoie, way up in the Rhône-Alpes, small Alpine cooperatives make this cheese immediately after milking, cooking it down in copper pots and binding the finished wheels in wooden hoops (look for the concave rind). You can find it as young as three months, but hold out for older wheels: The firm flesh is fruity and vegetal, without the razor sharpness of other mountain cheeses. A splurge for fondue, it goes nicely with a friendly Syrah.

AFFIDELICE

FRANCE | RAW/PASTEURIZED | WASHED RIND

A lesser-known, nose-kicking cousin of **Epoisses**, this Burgundy stinker is washed in the lively white wine Chablis, and the glossy, pale pink rind clings like a coat of Vaseline. Inside, the thick, buttery paste is both oozing liquid and moist cake. Don't try to eat around the rind: Just scoop the whole thing onto a slab of baguette. The barnyard aromas and bright orange hue come from the B. linens (*Brevibacterium linens*) that develop after repeated, salty washings. They may stain your fingers, but the rich, salty, fruity cream is delectable with a glass of crisp, steely Chablis or other white Burgundy.

AFUEGA'L PITU

SPAIN | RAW/PASTEURIZED | SEMISOFT

The Asturians don't call it "fire in the throat" for nothing. It may look like a delicate orange bulb, but the paprika rubdown that lends color also lends a smoky, fiery finish. Firm even in youth, with a light, lactic flavor that reminds us of dried sour cream, the knobby wheels mature to raucous pungency, with an insistent, astringent flavor to match. Typically found at one to two months of age, they become flaccid when they are overripe. Seek out a bold red, such as those from Rioja.

AISY CENDRÉ

FRANCE | RAW/PASTEURIZED | WASHED RIND

Don't go shaking any hands after you slice this up for your guests. The intense stink will stick to the fingers. The thick, oozing paste, comparable to

Epoisses, has a wondrous salty intensity without Epoisses's puckered, Day-Glo washed rind; rather, this Burgundian beauty is blanketed in downy gray ash. In the United States, a pasteurized version from Berthaut is the sole representative. Best enjoyed with the ash brushed off, it's harmonious with an austere Chardonnay from Burgundy.

ALPAGE PRATTIGAU

SWITZERLAND | RAW | FIRM

Pockmarked with olive-pit-sized holes and fragrant with the scent of hay and summer grasses, Alpage Prattigau is made in the summer months on a single alp in the Prattigau Valley. Each year, cows are herded in the mountains as the snow recedes, only to return to the valley each fall, in a long-standing cultural tradition known as transhumance. Tradition dictates the cheese is not to be consumed in its year of production, as a minimum of eight months' aging is necessary to develop exceptional texture and flavor. The firm, succulent paste is nutty, herbaceous, and full-flavored, with the soft sweetness of apricots. Scalded-milk flavors are pronounced, almost eggy. A guaranteed, if unexpected, pairing is with the dry, oxidized, toasted-nut richness of Oloroso sherry.

AMARELO DA BEIRA BAIXA

PORTUGAL | RAW | SEMISOFT | D.O.P.

This cheese may look like those soft, slurpy sheep cheeses from southern Spain, but it's not! A mixture of raw sheep and goat milk yields this semisoft, slightly unctuous round with a buttercup-yellow rind, named for the interior region of

Castelo Branco, Portugal, where it's produced. The clean, slightly acidic paste is rich and fatty. If you are silly enough not to finish it, after some time the cheese will get all oozy on you, and the cloth in which it's bound for support may get lost in the paste. Eat the cheese, not the cloth, along with a minerally white from the Rias Baixas.

ANTIGO CHEESE COMPANY STRAVECCHIO

USA | PASTEURIZED | HARD | VEGETARIAN

Remember the Antigans! In 1993, the owners of the Antigo cheese plant announced they would close the plant and move to more modern facilities. The people of Antigo—employees, milk patrons, and residents included—refused to let seventy years of cheesemaking history disappear. They pooled their resources, bought the plant, and, with master cheesemaker Larry Steckbauer at the helm, have been producing award-winning Parmesan-style cheeses ever since. Normally we shy away from domestically produced imitators of European greats, but Stravecchio is an exception: a dense, dry paste, with liberal pockets of crystalline crunch that taste of toasted nuts and pineapple. Intense and delicious. We like a hunk alongside California Zinfandel.

APPENZELLER

SWITZERLAND | RAW | FIRM

With seventy-five cooperatives cranking out some two hundred thousand wheels each year, there is good Appenzeller and not-so-good Appenzeller.

Avoid the foil-wrapped stuff that's firm but gummy and tastes like cheap slicing Swiss cheese. Smaller producers wash their wheels religiously in a brine of white wine or cider spiced with pepper and herbs. One producer we know of has a tub of brine that is thirty (that's no typo) years old. Continually topped off with fresh brew, that dank, spiced fruitiness pervades the cheese and lingers forever. Appenzeller is one of the three classic mountain cheeses (along with **Emmenthaler** and **Gruyère**) for unparalleled fondue. The spicy, floral aroma of Gewürztraminer, with its seductive fruit and bright acidity, only heightens the richness of this Swiss classic.

ARDI-GASNA

FRANCE | RAW | FIRM

This is the *fermier* version, made in the French Aquitaine, not the industrial Petit Basque that comes cloaked in wax. Complex and balanced with a thick, rustic rind that imparts a nutty flavor to the cheese, especially at its edges, it also has notes of caramel and coconut to round out the finish. This barrel-shaped cheese ranges in size from one to four kilograms; in the case of Petit Ardi-Gasna, expect a "small ewe cheese," the name's Basque translation. Traditionally, the rind was heated using embers from the fire, and the cheese was smeared with *bilgora* (sheep fat) to preserve it. We'll pass on the fat in favor of a bold red from Chile or Argentina, of the Malbec persuasion.

ARDRAHAN

IRELAND | PASTEURIZED | WASHED RIND

Mary Burns of county Cork is one of four remarkable women responsible for the resurrection of artisanal cheesemaking in Ireland. Her version of a washed rind is brushing a straightforward brine on a one-kilo wheel. Although the interior becomes runny after several months, we like this cheese young, when the core retains some chalkiness. The resulting textures are stiff cream and toothsome curd, the flavors rustic but balanced: saline, nearly smoky, with a pleasant whiff of wet earth. Too old and that runny center becomes ammoniated, acrid, and bitter. It's an ideal picnic cheese, paired with a hunk of fatty, cured meat. A thick, chocolaty stout tempers Ardrahan's masculinity. Guinness is our go-to choice.

ARZÚA ULLOA
(QUESO DE ARZÚA-ULLOA)

SPAIN | PASTEURIZED | SEMISOFT | D.O.

Holding a wheel of Arzúa is like grabbing the rolls of a baby's upper arm: thick, elastic, fatty softness. A more obscure Galacian cousin of **Tetilla**, Arzúa oozes creaminess, with just the right tang for balance. The rind is more like a thick skin, protecting a lactic, mouth-coating paste that has very little acidity or sharpness. An excellent breakfast cheese or melter for any occasion. If you need a drink, think local: Crisp Albariño is the perfect palate cleanser.

ASIAGO D'ALLEVO

ITALY | RAW | HARD | D.O.P.

This is mature, substantial Asiago—not young and soft like **Pressato** (see next entry)—with a longer aging period after the curd is cooked and pressed during production. Hailing from a parcel of Italy stretching from the Po River valley up to the northern alpine meadows, Asiago d'Allevo is best at eight to twelve months, though it's available as young as five. The pale caramel, oily rind protects a solid, straw-colored center that is piquant, savory, and rich with deep, cooked-milk flavor. This toothsome northern Italian table cheese brightens a plate of figs, grapes, and rustic bread; the clean fruit and nuttiness of Orvieto or Soave are affordable partners.

ASIAGO PRESSATO

ITALY | PASTEURIZED | SEMISOFT | D.O.P.

From the Po River valley to the northern Italian alpine meadows of the Veneto and Trentino-Alto Adige, you will find fresh, young Asiago Pressato. The pale, straw-yellow paste is soft and yielding, never sticky or greasy. Its aromas of yogurt and butter are a signpost to flavor: sweet and mild, lightly tangy, not overly rich or heavy. Try melting it over potatoes sprinkled with fresh herbs. Crisp, quaffable Pinot Grigio is appropriate for this simple, straightforward cheese.

AZEITÃO

PORTUGAL | RAW | SEMISOFT | VEGETARIAN | D.O.P.

This fat little disc, when ripe, has a succulent, melting, puddinglike interior and thin, yellow skin. Don't be misled by the indulgent texture: Luscious weightlessness does not mean an innocuous little blob. This is an *amanteigado* style, found only in southern Spain and Portugal, where cheese is co-agulated with cardoon thistle. The resulting flavors are piquant, slightly sour, vegetal, and floral. Love it or hate it, but try it, especially with thin slices of paprika-stained chorizo and a glass or two of Portuguese Douro.

BANON

FRANCE | RAW | FRESH | A.O.C.

The real McCoy from Provence is hard to find here, because by French law it must be made with raw milk, and it simply can't last the necessary sixty days to be legal; you'll often see pasteurized rip-offs made of cow's milk. If you can find the real deal, you might expect that a disc of fresh goat cheese, neatly wrapped in a chestnut leaf and bound with raffia, would be a bland, creamy little bit of nothing special. Wrong! The desiccation of the leaf wrapper—traditionally macerated in wine, eau-de-vie, or marc—imparts a sharp, woody fla-vor that can be quite strong. Look for a fresh green leaf if you prefer young, tart cheese. The older the wrapper (dry and brown), the stronger the cheese. Soften it with fruit: cherries and berries to eat whole, or grapes in a bottle of juicy Provençal rosé.

BASKET CHEESE

ITALY | PASTEURIZED | FRESH

A quintessential fresh cheese, basket cheese is not unlike ricotta, though it's made from whole milk rather than whey. This Italian American staple is traditionally served in Easter Sunday ham pie. It's also a superb example of the simple goodness of fresh cheese; unlike those made from goat's milk, with their lemony tang, the cow's-milk versions are smooth, luscious, and milky. There's no need to wait for Easter. A perfect summertime dessert drizzled with a bit of honey and served with a flute of Prosecco.

BEAUFORT D'ALPAGE

FRANCE | RAW | FIRM | A.O.C.

Eighteenth-century French gastronome Brillat-Savarin called it the "Prince of Gruyères," and it remains one of the most impressive traditional cheeses available. (It's important to note that although there are similarities between Beaufort and Swiss **Gruyère**, they are not the same; in fact, in France, *gruyère* is the generic term for large cooked, pressed cheeses.) Made for a few millennia, this cheese received its A.O.C. status in 1976. The concave sides of each enormous eighty-five-pound wheel provide the perfect track for a cord with which the cheese is strapped to a donkey's back for a lumbering journey down into valley towns. It is made exclusively from the milk of a single herd of cows that graze on Alpine meadows across the mountainous region of Savoie. The rarest kind of Beaufort, Beaufort d'Alpage must be made between June and October, when thousands of tiny flowers, grasses, and clover unique to the Alps bestow aromas and flavors of cooked fruit, butter, cream, hay, and hazelnuts. Seek this dense, hearty cheese in winter, when wheels have had at least eight months of cold cellar ripening, and its rich beefiness so well suits those cold, windy nights. Savor it with that '82 Bordeaux you've been saving, or perhaps an Oregon Pinot Noir.

BEENLEIGH BLUE

ENGLAND | PASTEURIZED | BLUE | VEGETARIAN

At Sharpham Barton, near Devon, Robin Congdon and Nick Trant produce one of the finest sheep's-milk blues in the world. While the rich fat of the paste is mellow and fudgy, Beenleigh differs from their other signature cheeses, **Harbourne Blue** and **Ticklemore**, in its propensity for fierceness with age. That dense, white paste maintains its burnt-caramel depth, but the thin threads of blue deepen in pepper and intensity at around six months. The contrast of sweet and spice is ideal alongside a glass of sweet, late-harvest wine, from Sauternes to Riesling.

BELLWETHER FARM CARMODY (RESERVE)

USA | RAW/PASTEURIZED | FIRM | VEGETARIAN

Twice a week, the Callahan family of Petaluma, California, travels three miles to a neighboring farm to collect five hundred to eight hundred gallons of the purest Jersey cow's milk to make their unique Carmody, with either pasteurized or raw milk (Reserve). Firm, hearty, and mild, it makes an ideal table cheese. Don't expect intense sharpness or nuttiness; instead, anticipate butter-yellow milk condensed to a grassy finish. Put it out for a buffet lunch spread with coarse bread, olives, sliced meats, and a bottle of California Chardonnay.

BELLWETHER FARM SAN ANDREAS

USA | RAW | FIRM

Liam Callahan makes cheese from the milk of the family's flock of two hundred East Friesian sheep. His mother, Cindy, shepherds the flock that grazes on the rolling hills of Petaluma, California. The mellow sheep produce clean, fatty, tangy milk, which Liam transforms into a sweet, mild, aged cheese with no sheepy (read: gamy, "dirty-animal") flavor. The waxy yellow rind doesn't make for good eating, but the dense, butter-crumble paste is the perfect foil for the lush, spicy smoke of a northern California or Oregon Pinot Noir.

BERKSWELL

ENGLAND | RAW | HARD | VEGETARIAN

Located in the West Midlands of England, the Fletcher family's Ram Hall Dairy has taken a staple of the Italian table (**Pecorino**) and turned it into a revelation. Though the paste is firm, even crumbly, your mouth can feel the fat. And though it is milder in flavor than most sheep cheeses, you can taste the impeccably balanced notes of clover, hazelnut, and hay. The finish is lush with the sweetness of fresh cream. Argentinian Malbec offers the smoothness of Merlot without fear of excessive fruit-juiciness that can drown Berkswell's subtleties.

BETHMALE

FRANCE | RAW/PASTEURIZED | SEMISOFT

The Pyrénées are the land of sheep, yet here is the region's best-known traditional wheel from cow's milk. Named for the village of its production, Bethmale is veritably glossy with fat when you cut into its firm, golden rind. Mild and rich, the finish is savory, especially after some months of cave maturation. Pasteurized versions lack all nuance and tend toward gumminess. Find the raw, and serve it with a glass of Syrah or Bordeaux alongside.

BISHOP KENNEDY

SCOTLAND | PASTEURIZED | WASHED RIND

Named for the founder of the United Colleges of St. Andrews in the fifteenth century who likely enjoyed a nip of malt whiskey, this namesake cheese is bathed in the stuff until it softens to an aggressively aromatic puddle. Made by the folks at Howgate Farm in Perthshire, Scotland, Bishop Kennedy is best with a pint of stout, or a fine single malt in honor of the Bishop. Both emphasize the vegetal, peat moss intensity of the finish.

BITTERSWEET PLANTATION DAIRY EVANGELINE

USA | PASTEURIZED | BLOOMY | VEGETARIAN

Take a pillowy little drum of goat's-milk cheese infused with cream, and you get the whipped, buttery indulgence of 75 percent butterfat. Hailing from Gonzales, Louisiana, in Cajun country, Evangeline is one of only three triple-crème goats we

know of. The intense richness is offset by a characteristic tang known (not so helpfully) as "goatiness." It's that little mouthwatery, citrus-sparkly bite
found in many goat cheeses. Cut the buttery
mouthfeel with thinly sliced fresh strawberries, great
for offsetting the salt. Serve with Chenin Blanc.

BITTERSWEET PLANTATION DAIRY FLEUR-DE-LIS

USA | PASTEURIZED | BLOOMY | VEGETARIAN

In Gonzales, Louisiana, a mere hour outside New
Orleans, cream-infused Guernsey cow's milk
takes two weeks to mature into these bell-shaped
delicacies. With a thin skin of soft, edible, blooming rind, the paste inside remains ever so dense,
but dissolves instantly on the tongue into salt-
cream-milkiness. It is appropriately named for the
national symbol of France, because the French
were the first Europeans to settle Louisiana. For
variety, the cheesemaker also offers Fleur-de-
Teche, with a decorative line of vegetable ash
across the middle. As with all triple-crèmes, we
prefer Champagne or another effervescent mouthful such as sweet Moscato d'Asti to froth against
the mouth-coating cream.

BITTO

ITALY | RAW | FIRM | D.O.P.

The strict production methods of Bitto state that it
can be made only during the summer months, when
cows feast on high mountain grasses and cheese is
produced by hand in small stone huts known as
calecc. Though the cheese may contain up to 10
percent goat's milk, Murray's prefers wheels that are

entirely raw cow, with a thin, hard, straw-colored rind and fine, firm paste heady with aromas of grass and cooked milk. With longer aging, the paste dries to a piquant, tangy, and long biting finish. Produced in Italy's northern region of Lombardy, Bitto is well suited to fruity red Valpolicella.

BLEU D'AUVERGNE

FRANCE | RAW/PASTEURIZED | BLUE | A.O.C.

With good reason, Bleu d'Auvergne inspires regional pride. The Auvergnats claim that this cheese originated in the mid-nineteenth century, when a shepherd added blue mold from rye bread to a wheel of cheese and pierced the wheel to allow the mold to flourish. Of course, the story goes, he did this before any shepherd in nearby Roquefort could do the same thing, so *this* blue cheese is the true French classic. With a firm but creamy texture, perfectly integrated blue veining, and a medium-strength spiciness, it's excellent crumbled over salad or drizzled with chestnut honey. Given the choice, we'd opt for a sweet wine to offset the salt, be it port or Sauternes. If you're finishing a bottle of red, let's hope it's the dried-cranberry spice of an Aussie Shiraz.

BLEU DE TERMIGNON

FRANCE | RAW | BLUE

There are only three cheesemakers still producing this rare French variant of **Castelmagno**, made in the high mountain pastures of the Haute-Savoie. The firm, crumbly, almost sandy paste blues naturally when exposed to air, so young wheels often have no blueing at all. The lactic, yogurt flavors of younger cheese are stunningly floral, though they sharpen and intensify, with a peppery and pervasive finish, as blue mold develops. We predict extinction in the next decade, so if you find it, savor it with good company and a nuanced French Burgundy.

BLEU DU HAUT-JURA (BLEU DE GEX)

FRANCE | RAW | BLUE | A.O.C.

One of France's oldest and least-altered blues happens to be a great choice for those who don't like blue. Unusually large wheels weighing about ten pounds indicate the Alpine origins of this cheese from the Jura, located on the Swiss border, and home of the giant cheese wheels. It is worth noting that the official A.O.C. name is Bleu du Haut-Jura, although in the United States it is most commonly sold as Bleu de Gex, and less commonly as Bleu de Septmoncel. Made from the milk of high-altitude-grazing Montbellarde cows, inoculated with the mild blue mold *Penicillium glaucum*, and syringe-injected with air to promote the mold's propagation, the wheels have a soft sweetness that is complemented by some horsey, leathery aromas. With its protective rind, the cheese can age for longer periods of time and retain a moist pliability, which some have called gummy. Light, sweet wines with simple fruit, like Muscat, are ideal.

BOERENKAAS

See **Gouda**

BRA TENERO OR DURO

ITALY | RAW/PASTEURIZED | SEMISOFT OR FIRM | D.O.P.

Taking its name from the town near Turin, not lingerie, this name-protected cheese comes in both Tenero (young) and Duro (aged) versions. Bland, commercial versions are produced from pasteurized milk, cut with some goat and sheep milk, but the authentic versions are 100 percent grass-fed bovine. Tenero, aged for less than two months and somewhat spongy, is unremarkable but perfectly pleasant, with a fresh buttermilk flavor. Things get interesting after six months, as Tenero develops a hard beige rind and compact paste riddled with small holes. That buttermilk sourness intensifies, and offers an intense but altogether different flavor from the cooked-milk, sweet-nutty sharpness of French or Swiss mountain cheeses. The robust reds of this Nebbiolo-heavy area suit perfectly. Or seek out a slightly lighter Dolcetto.

BRESCIANELLA STAGIONATA

ITALY | RAW | WASHED RIND

You might mistake this rare find from Lombardy for a mini-square of **Taleggio**. Brine washed for four to six weeks, it is strong on the nose but easy on the mouth: creamy, sweet, and yeasty, with the addictive flavor of perfectly salted, freshly baked bread. This cow's milk cheese is a great introduction to the world of stinky cheese—try it before graduating to versions described as bacony, noxious, or barny. The omnipresent, crisp, and relatively simple Italian white Pinot Grigio is a choice starter companion.

BRIE

FRANCE | RAW/PASTEURIZED | BLOOMY

Every supermarket in America has Brie in one form or another, and the name doesn't guarantee very much except a bloomy rind and a butterfat content of 50 percent (well, then there's that "Lite" Brie we'll pretend we didn't see). Look for varieties imported from France. Canadian or German origins don't count any more than the stuff made domestically. Also keep an eye out for superior 60 percent butterfat versions. Know you're going to eat something pretty bland, albeit consistent. Creamy, buttery, and soft, it has a bright white rind that can have a sharp, somewhat plasticky flavor. Brie is not likely to offend—unless it smells very strongly of ammonia, in which case the cheese has "gone by" and should be thrown away. Also, it bears no resemblance to the true great name-protected Bries of France (see following entries). For nibbles before dinner, opt for a straightforward red or white wine without excessive tannins. A California Merlot or Chardonnay will please everyone.

BRIE DE MEAUX

FRANCE | RAW | BLOOMY | A.O.C.

For every gourmet who scoffed at Brie as boring, for every enthusiast who wondered what the big deal about Brie is, this is the big deal! As defined by its legal protection, it must be made from raw milk, and how profound the difference. The smooth, straw-colored paste is complex and assertive, with a lovely, spicy aftertaste reminiscent of mushrooms and black truffles—earthy, sexy, and luscious. The characteristic runniness develops as it ripens. This real deal is made from the milk of cows grazing on the lush pasturage outside of Paris in Ile-de-France.

The difficulty in finding this divine raw milk cheese, so rarely aged the legal sixty days, drives us to champion the more easily available but pasteurized **Fromage de Meaux**.

BRIE DE MELUN 🐄
FRANCE | RAW | BLOOMY | A.O.C.

If you see a wheel in France you may think it's just an old, slightly sticky wheel of **Brie de Meaux**. And though it's made in the same region of Ile-de-France, you're looking at an entirely different beast. Unlike Meaux, these wheels undergo lactic coagulation, meaning minimal rennet is added, and the cheese coagulates over many hours (by law at least eighteen) as starter cultures acidify the milk. This, coupled with a seven- to ten-week maturation time, produces an uneven, brownish crust protecting a strong, robust, slightly salty paste. It makes Meaux seem positively refined. Sip a Pinot Noir for balance.

BRIE DE NANGIS 🐄
FRANCE | PASTEURIZED | BLOOMY

This smaller round is a pasteurized take on **Brie de Meaux**, though laudable cheesemaking means a wheel that retains flavor and complexity. The paste is firmer than we'd like, but admirably milky and sweet. Give it time and it will break down into near-liquidity, smacking of savory mushroom and moist black truffle. From the Brie capital, Ile-de-France, it's easier to find than Meaux.

FROMAGE DE MEAUX 🐄

FRANCE | PASTEURIZED | BLOOMY

This knockoff of A.O.C. **Brie de Meaux** is created primarily for an export market that requires pasteurized milk, such as the United States. But, hey, if Karl Lagerfeld can make Chanel for H&M at $12, then the French can make a decent pasteurized cheese. And this is better than decent: it's great, at its best almost as good as the real thing, with slippery, melting insides and that addictive mushroom/truffle combo. Watch for unscrupulous cheesemongers selling this as Brie de Meaux: If it seems cheap and readily available, it is too good to be true.

The depth and nuance of these silken cheeses calls for a wine with earth and spice. The famed reds of the Côtes du Rhône are ideal; try Châteauneuf-du-Pape for a splurge.

BRILLAT-SAVARIN 🐄

FRANCE | RAW/PASTEURIZED | BLOOMY

Two hundred years after French gastronome Brillat-Savarin waxed poetic about the sensual pleasures of cheese, Normandy cheesemaker Henri Androuët created a sinful, fatty delicacy in his honor. His son Pierre carries on the tradition of full-fat cheese. With a thin, edible, snowy rind and a mousselike interior, this airy delicacy is enriched with cream for voluptuous, mouth-coating satisfaction. The mark of a fine triple-crème is its ability to enter your mouth as a savory slab of seemingly dense cake and instantly dissolve into creamy liquidity, with no trace of ammonia. This one does it every time. Cut that fat with bubbles, from California to Champagne to Italian Prosecco.

BRIN D'AMOUR

FRANCE | RAW/PASTEURIZED | SEMISOFT

The sweet, supple block that put Corsica on the cheesemaking map. Similar to its twin sister, **Fleur du Maquis**, this "bit of love" is covered with an intensely aromatic blend of rosemary, savory, chile pepper, and juniper berry, evoking the sunbaked, rocky ledges and scrub brush that grows near the Mediterranean. The age of this cheese, like that of **Banon**, can be identified by the color and freshness of the herbage covering it. When the herbs are bright and green, the cheese is creamy and clean with the light tang of sour cream; when the herbs have turned brown, the fine-textured interior softens under the herbaceous crust, exposing a perimeter that is quite runny. At this point in its maturity, the aroma is deep, almost biting, on the inhalation. Light, soft white wines such as California Fumé Blanc or the bracing acidity of French Sauvignon Blanc both marry well with this aromatic cheese.

BUCHERON

FRANCE | PASTEURIZED | BLOOMY

Bûcheron means lumberjack, woodcutter, logger. The cheese is a log-shaped bauble, offering the opportunity to try goat cheese with some age and complexity. The mold-ripened rind cloaks a thin layer, like soft, beaten butter, just underneath. The very center is chalky, almost flaky, and bright white. A classic choice to top a tangle of spring greens, it is one of the more accessible and common French chèvres found in American shops. Stay in step with a high-acid white wine that's never touched oak, like the classic Sauvignon Blancs of France's Loire Valley, due north of Poitou, where Bucheron is made.

BURRATA
See **Mozzarella**

CABRA PENAMACOR
PORTUGAL | RAW | WASHED RIND

That bright white paste declares this cheese's goaty origins, and on the tongue it's like **feta**, or dried cheese curds that break into little niblets under the slightest pressure. Sure enough, the raw milk is a bounty of flavor, highly acidic but sweet, with a woodsy quality not unlike our favorite **Garrotxa**. From the mountains of central Portugal, and aged for a mere two months, that surly orange rind has a kick of salt and no small amount of fruitiness that is well coupled with mouthwateringly crisp Vinho Verde.

CABRALES (QUESO CABRALES)
OR MIXED (COW WITH SMALL AMOUNTS OF GOAT, SHEEP, OR A COMBINATION) | SPAIN | RAW | BLUE | D.O.

Several different blues are made in the Picos de Europa of northern Spain, and many are mistakenly sold under the legally protected Cabrales name. True Cabrales is still a farmhouse cheese, with seasonal variation and fleeting availability. The milk of cows (and sometimes goats and sheep, depending on availability) grazing on high-altitude pastures is formed into wheels and aged one month, followed by at least two additional months in natural limestone caves. Originally wrapped in sycamore leaves, Cabrales is now found covered in foil, with a logo stamped into it to prove its origin. The interior mold may develop spontaneously with exposure to air; because the cheese is not inoculated with blue mold spores, don't expect a neat web of blue veining. Mature Cabrales has the peculiar gray-green color of Yoda's skin, with a sandy, crumbling texture. It is a deliciously strong, fierce, eye-watering, throat-searing, mouth-numbing experience. To pair with a blue, we usually like a dessert wine that's got balance and acidity, but Cabrales can stand up to the thick, oily sweetness of Spanish Pedro Ximénez (PX) sherry.

CACIOCAVALLO SILANO

ITALY | RAW/PASTEURIZED | FIRM | D.O.P.

These taut, oiled, gourd-shaped balls are most often hung for impressive display beside whole legs of prosciutto and torpedoes of fat-studded salami at Italian groceries in New York. That Murray's carries Caciocavallo at all speaks to the Italian roots of our West Village block of Manhattan. Despite the indications of its name (*cacio* = cheese, *cavallo* = horse), the cheese is not made from mare's milk. The name refers to the method of aging Caciocavallo, where a pair of cheeses are tied with rope and strung over a beam, as if astride a horse. While Caciocavallo has been made in numerous Italian districts in the Campania, Calabria, and Molise regions since the Middle Ages, the only ones that receive name protection (D.O.P.) are made in the region of Calabria. Our highest recommendation goes to those made from raw milk, but if you find a very mature, pasteurized Caciocavallo, it will also be worth your while: Expect this *pasta filata* cheese (pulled and stretched like mozzarella) to be aged to a salty, spicy finish, not unlike aged provolone. Its melting capabilities are excellent and its flavor is rustic, full, and mellow, with a lingering bite at the end. If you were to dare to buy Chianti in those straw-covered casks, this would be the cheese to serve with it.

CAERPHILLY

WALES | RAW/PASTEURIZED | SEMISOFT

Caerphilly is known as a Welsh cheese, but this is not the whole story. Made in and around Cardiff since at least the 1830s, it was a favorite lunchtime cheese for Welsh miners. Back then, it was aged far longer than wheels are today, until the paste was brown and the flavor intense and salty. So popular was Caerphilly that English cheesemakers began their own production, virtually destroying the market for the real Welsh-made version. Not until after World War II did production resume. Today, there are several industrial producers churning out bland, pasteurized dreck. Seek out our preferred Gorwydd. Some traditionalists bemoan the modern, milky, youthful version while others prefer its soft, tart flavor and moist, cakey paste. Each light, citrusy bite goes down well with a lemony wheat beer. We like Hoegaarden.

CAMEMBERT DE NORMANDIE

FRANCE | RAW | BLOOMY | A.O.C.

The story of the origin of this cheese has suffered a persistent run through the rumor mill. According to legend, during the French Revolution, Camembert (the town) resident Marie Harel provided shelter to a Roman Catholic priest in exile from Brie. In exchange for sanctuary, he gave her the recipe for Camembert. That's the legend. In fact, the cheese has been made in Camembert since the mid-1500s. In 1850, the advent of railroads delivered Camembert to Paris, where, in 1855, the press reported that Napoleon was so overwhelmed by Camembert's succulence that he jumped from his seat and kissed the serving maid. On a more utilitarian note, in 1890, the ubiquitous round wooden box was invented for Camembert to protect it during its train rides.

By law it's raw, and for a reason. Tucked away in its neat wooden box, liquid ecstasy awaits. Beneath a soft, yielding, furry white rind, true ripe Camembert is slurpy, soothing, mushroomy perfection. Squeeze the cheese: It should feel like the webbing between your itching fingers as you tear off the paper wrapper to consume the treasure within. Ammonia's no good; rather, the aromas of melted butter, wet straw, and damp fungus should waft into the room. Stay simple with the wines; Camembert is too good to mess with. A glass of Côtes du Rhône or an earthy white goes best. If you can't find the raw version (it's gonna be tricky), seek out Camembert Châtelain, wrapped in paper, not plastic: It's an impressive pasteurized version.

CAPRA VALTELLINA

ITALY | PASTEURIZED | FIRM

Another succinctly named cheese from the Italians: *Capra* means "goat," *Valtellina* refers to the mountainous region in northern Italy, and it all adds up to "a goat cheese from Valtellina." This one is an atypical goat cheese, especially for Italians, with its firm texture and saline, grassy, herbaceous flavor. Although it can be quite mild, when you hit this cheese at the right age (at least five months) it can taste downright woodsy, with strong aromas of Christmas tree. Even then, it's delicate and likes a quiet wine, like Italian Orvieto.

CAPRINO NOCE

ITALY | RAW | FRESH

A sturdy drum of fluffy, airy cheese wrapped in a damp black walnut leaf equates to springtime eating bliss in Piedmont, or wherever you happen to be. This seasonal delicacy offers a fungal, woody counterpoint to the typically zesty citrus flavors of fresh goat cheese. Bound with a bit of hay, each little package gives the gift of goatdom: perfectly balanced, tart, and twiggy. We're going to veer away from the standard Sauvignon Blanc pairing and go light, red, and local, in the form of Barbera.

CAPRIOLE FARM O'BANON

USA | PASTEURIZED | FRESH

Oh, baby, this ain't no French **Banon**. Judy Schad, a pioneering American producer, cranks out O'Banon in Greenville, Indiana, using the milk of her herd of free-roaming goats. As you already know, Provençal Banon is traditionally washed in eau-de-vie before being wrapped in chestnut leaves. Judy makes a slightly larger round of cheese and wraps it in leaves doused with good Kentucky bourbon: Old Forester or Woodford Reserve are the producers of choice. The tannins in the leaves and bourbon give a good kick to the otherwise dense, creamy, milky puck. For the strong, a tumbler of Woodford complements the woody flavors.

CASHEL BLUE

IRELAND | PASTEURIZED | BLUE | VEGETARIAN

Some events are a blessing in disguise. Consider the Grubb family, kicked out of England three hundred years ago for Anabaptist tendencies. They relocated to Fethard, in county Tipperary, Ireland, and took up buttermaking, a dairy heritage continued by Louis and Jane Grubb today. Luckily for us, in addition to butter, they are also making this sumptuous, mellow, creamy blue. At its prime, we've found Cashel to be as hearty as smoked meat, but always milky, without the intense, metallic punch that turns so many off blue cheese. If that's not enough reason for Cashel to end up on your cheese board, consider this: It's the first farmstead blue made in Ireland. So get yourself a tiny glass of Oloroso sherry or a tawny port and eat a bit of history.

CASTELMAGNO

ITALY | RAW | SEMISOFT | D.O.P.

Despite **Parmigiano-Reggiano**'s international fame, some consider *this* the "King of Italian Cheese." The traditional manner in which it is produced and a recorded history dating to 1277 makes Castelmagno the pride of Piedmont cheese production. A tall, dense cylinder of white-just-this-side-of-gray paste with a firm and flaky texture, Castelmagno is sheathed in a strange and beautiful rind covered with powdery red, yellow, white, and gray molds. The flavor is as nuanced as the rind: milky, slightly saline, and pleasantly lactic. With age, expect a drier, sandy paste and sharper mushroom finish. Barbaresco is the ticket for pairing with this Formaggio Rex.

CASTELROSSO

ITALY | PASTEURIZED | SEMISOFT

Here's a pasteurized Italian knockoff of **Castelmagno**, also Piedmontese. We find that many Americans prefer the softer, creamier paste of Castelrosso. It's got the same thick, molded, earth-smelling rind. But the paste just beneath breaks down into luscious, thick cream, while the inner core remains chalky and lactic. On the whole, it's mushroomy, but also tangy, with the heft of cold butter. Taste it next to Castelmagno, and see what you think. And enjoy that beautiful Barbera with both.

CATO CORNER BRIDGID'S ABBEY

USA | RAW | SEMISOFT

Colchester, Connecticut, is home to the mother-son partnership of Elizabeth MacAlister and Mark Gillman, whose sustainable agricultural practices include the regular fertilizing of fields with whey, the liquid by-product of cheesemaking. Their herd of Jersey cows is rotationally grazed on this thick, lush pasturage, and this cheese is named for the patron saint of cheesemaking. Bridgid's Abbey has a coarse, stone-colored rind that protects a pliable, buttery paste tasting of clover and tangy buttermilk; it's aged at least four months for a pronounced yet gentle flavor. This is a real "eating cheese," ideal for sandwiches, summer lunches, or slicing with tart, local apples. Add a bottle of Merlot and make the treat complete.

CATO CORNER DRUNKEN HOOLIGAN

USA | RAW | WASHED RIND

Mothers, take comfort: We speak not of your sons. Mark Gillman's rascally Hooligan wasn't enough—he had to go and dunk it in the grape must left over from a neighbor's winemaking. Seasonally produced, when there's grape skin and stick left over, this Hooligan carries all the rough tannins and brusque body you avoid in a drinking red. With the rich texture of superfat Jersey cow's milk, you also get the coarse, peppery fruit flavors of rustic red wine. Gang up on this cheese with a carafe of Valpolicella and some drunken hooligans.

CATO CORNER DRUNK MONK

USA | RAW | WASHED RIND

One of cheesemaker Mark Gillman's seasonal variations on **Hooligan**, this creation is washed in local ale, rather than the straight-up brine used for Hooligan. The difference between the two is the fermented fruitiness that characterizes each fat little wheel. Try it with a pint of IPA (India pale ale) or any other fruity microbrew—you'll be sure to enjoy the long, lingering, sticky paste. And you'll definitely get a buzz on.

CATO CORNER HOOLIGAN

USA | RAW | WASHED RIND

Remember the sixty-day raw milk rule? This handsome round is barely legal—two months of age—when the grainy, tangerine rind is soft and yielding. Washed in buttermilk and brine, the sticky, uniform paste has a long, barnyardy finish. Grass-fed Jersey cows mean the character and texture change throughout the year. We like it best in the winter months, when the fat content is higher, the wheels slippery and bulging. Summer cheese is firmer, but more varied in flavor: Wild herbs impart hints of licorice and anise. Partner this Hooligan with a heady monastery brew like Chimay.

CHABICHOU DU POITOU

FRANCE | RAW | SEMISOFT | A.O.C.

Think goat cheese is animally? This perfect cylinder sheathed in a ridged rind, peppered with patches of blue and white mold, will change your mind. Have no fear, it's all good, down to the dense, Arctic-white center: sweet, slightly minerally, and clean. Do yourself the favor of avoiding this cheese from December through March, when the delectable claylike insides become rubbery and Gumby-fied. Winter isn't the time for goat's milk, and this little guy is worth waiting for. Drink regionally, seeking out white wines from Poitou or the nearby celebrated whites of the Loire Valley. These classic Sauvignon Blancs are appropriately crisp and grassy.

CHAOURCE

FRANCE | RAW/PASTEURIZED | BLOOMY | A.O.C.

A sturdy drum with the so-bad-it's-good flavor of buttered movie-theater popcorn, named after the town of its origin. It's got just a bit more butterfat content than **Brie**, bringing it above 50 percent fat in dry matter, but still not quite enough to rank it as a double-crème (60 to 74 percent), for which it is commonly mistaken. Chaource is drier than most bloomy-rinded cheeses; the flaking interior has been known to slide out of the rind if left at room temperature for more than a few hours. No matter, simply stuff it back in and eat quickly. With a history dating back to the seventh century, this venerable dairy product has a well-established track record satisfying the hunger for mild, buttery, decadent foodstuffs. From the region of Champagne-Ardenne, it should obviously be nibbled with none other than dry, yeasty Champagne.

CHAROLLAIS

FRANCE | RAW | SEMISOFT

If Chabichou is the sweet, pudgy nephew, Charollais is the austere great-aunt. Not boring or undesirable, mind you, but refined. Another small cylinder, this time from Burgundy, Charollais presents a crinkled almond rind; when in season, from April through October, she livens up, with a silky, moist skirt surrounding her slightly crumbling interior. With age, she becomes a bit drier, more assertive, snappy, but always bright and mown-grassy. Stay regional with the dry Chardonnay-based wines of northern Burgundy.

CHEDDAR, ENGLISH FARMHOUSE

ENGLAND | RAW | FIRM

Walk into any supermarket, and chances are good you'll find a wide selection of Cheddars. Unfortunately, most of them will either blaze orange through Cryovac, or they will sit under a heavy layer of wax. Because Cheddar has no name protection, any gummy block can come by this name. *Cheddar* comes from the cheesemaking method of "cheddaring," wherein curds are cut into blocks and stacked to exude whey. While the supermarket choices may be cheddared, they bear no resemblance to real Cheddar.

Look to the dairy farmers of Somerset, producing raw milk wheels aged in cheesecloth and cut to order from big fifty-six-pound wheels. Real English Cheddar won't arrive in logs, blocks, or bricks; when cut down from a wheel, it will take the form of a wedge. Cheddar is so important to the English palate that during World War II, it was illegal to produce any other variety of cheese, other than for personal consumption. Our favorites follow, and the variety in flavor profile, even within this narrowly defined group, is staggering.

KEEN'S

ENGLAND | RAW | FIRM

Compared with **Montgomery's Cheddar** (see next entry) and its three-hundred-year history, Keen's is just a teenager. Produced at Moorhayes Farm in Somerset since 1899 by the Keen family, it is currently being made by brothers Stephen and George Keen, and their sons Nick and James. With 210 Friesian cows and a dedication to farmstead production, this tiny company continues to churn out superb cloth-bound Cheddar. The pale straw-yellow paste has pronounced vegetal notes and pretty intense acidity (sharpness), undercutting the slight bitterness of almonds. Of the farmhouse Cheddars we know, Keen's is the one most likely to please that guy who wants the sharpest thing you've got, only with nuance. He will also like beer with his Cheddar—a straightforward brown ale like Newcastle.

MONTGOMERY'S

ENGLAND | RAW | FIRM

The English have regularly bestowed upon Montgomery's the title of Best Cheddar in the World, which is saying a lot. Made by Jamie Montgomery from sweet Friesian cow's milk, each wheel is aged in cloth and brushed with lard every few days, resulting in a firm but crumbly paste that breaks apart in the mouth, lodges in the teeth, and slowly releases the perfectly balanced taste of dried fig and almond. Barely sharp, with just enough balance for the measured fat and salt, it has a pleasant musty grassiness just beneath the rind. Serve fruit chutney with a kick of spice to emphasize this Cheddar's myriad flavors. Enjoy with a Cabernet Sauvignon made anywhere from France to California to Chile.

QUICKE'S

ENGLAND | RAW/PASTEURIZED | FIRM

Mary Quicke oversees a herd of 340 cross-bred cows in Devon: Holstein/Friesian cows and Friesian/Ayrshire cows that spend ten months a year eating grass for the richest, most flavorful milk possible in her cloth-bound Cheddar. When the cows are off grass, very little cheese is made, the intention being to control flavor and quality by minimizing production from the milk of cows fed on silage. Mary's is the most rustic farmhouse Cheddar we've found, with strong hay and earth aromas (think pleasantly dank cellar), a firm paste, and, as an ideal mature Cheddar should have, more flavor and less acidity (sharpness) than "sharp Cheddar." It's our favorite for the Cheddar connoisseur, and we have developed a specific flavor profile and age for all wheels sent to Murray's. Quicke's is best with a juicy red like Merlot.

CHESHIRE

ENGLAND | RAW/PASTEURIZED | FIRM

A distant cousin of **Cheddar** that's often mistaken for it, Cheshire is truly its own cheese. Thought to be the first named cheese made in England, Cheshire was once the name for generic English cheese; sixty years ago, at least four hundred farms were making it. Today, there are a few commodity (a.k.a. factory) producers of Cheshire, and one singular traditional farmstead producer, Mrs. Lucy Appleby. Making cheese for at least half a century, she says the family's cheesemaking techniques are "run by the curd, not the clock." This isn't the plastic-wrapped block you may know, but a cloth-bound, crumby, saline masterpiece of mild, buttery depth. Pale orange in color, it's easy on the eyes as well as on the palate. If you are a Cheddar lover, try this variation; the trademark lemony finish won't disappoint. Small-production cheese needs microbrewed beer. We happily marry Mrs. Appleby's with Magic Hat's spunky Fat Angel. Call it Fat Appleby.

CHÈVRE NOIR

CANADA | PASTEURIZED | HARD

When someone comes along peddling a "goat **Cheddar**," we are suspicious. Why mess with a great thing? In this case, the unexpected can offer a new level of greatness. Québec's Fromagerie Tournevant managed just that: a hard, chalk-white cheese with an insanely long, winey finish and delightful clusters of crunch. Yes, it's pasteurized, but this cheesemaker follows the treatise of "if you're going to do it, do it right." Whereas most cheesemakers will pasteurize their milk by rapidly bringing it to a very high temperature, thus "cooking out" the nuances, Tournevant uses milk that has been pasteurized *slowly*, and at a lower temperature, thus preserving the sweet complexity we demand in a great Cheddar. Emphasize that finish with a mouthful of bright raspberry: Gamay-based Chinon to impress your friends, or any Beaujolais.

CHEVROT

FRANCE | PASTEURIZED | SEMISOFT

If the delights of **Chabichou du Poitou** and **Charollais** prove elusive in your local market (and in their rarity it is possible they will), turn to the more industrial, but reliably delicious Chevrot. Looking like a squat, wrinkled drum, Chevrot at its best is plump, moist, and creamy. Its ridged rind, the result of the mold Geotrichum candidum, is fully edible, as is the sweet, tangy, claylike paste. From Poitou, in the Loire Valley, it's a great "starter goat," with some nuance and complexity but never an aggressive animal flavor. Beautiful with crisp Sauvignon Blanc or grassy Spanish Albariño.

CHEVROTIN (FORMERLY CHEVROTIN DES ARAVIS)

FRANCE | RAW | WASHED RIND | A.O.C.

When Savoie shepherds move their herds of cows into the Alps for summer grazing, the goats are sent up first to clear the trails. Some brilliant up-start figured it wouldn't be a bad idea to milk these goats that must now, by law, feast on Alpine grass and hay at least five months a year. These are cheesemakers with generations of experience crafting that inimitable cheese **Reblochon**. Here, they've created a phenomenal variation: a minia-ture Reblochon made of goat's milk. Small saucers are hand washed in brine to promote a sticky, yielding exterior and a supple, piquant, barnyardy paste. A stinky goat is common; a stinky goat's-milk cheese is a rare delicacy, best enjoyed with Loire whites or a German Riesling.

CHIABRO D'HENRY

ITALY | RAW | FIRM

From a region that produces some of the world's greatest red wine comes this impressive cheese, which is rubbed and smeared with the grape must (skins and seeds) from that wine production. This *ubriaco* (drunk) style of cheese is usually made from cow's milk in Italy's northeastern Veneto region. Here is a brilliant Piedmontese exception: raw goat, stark white against its nubbly, crusty coating of recycled grape bits. Its tempting flavor retains the integrity of tart, tangy goat cheese. Fruity, to be sure, but not artificially grapey, it is a seasonal delicacy made after the grape harvest. In keeping with the cheese's origin, think Barbaresco from Piedmont.

CHIMAY

BELGIUM | RAW/PASTEURIZED | WASHED RIND

Take a building full of keg-tapping monks, and you wind up with Chimay. Historically, this is the origin of most washed rinds, as monasteries were the original producers of wine and beer. It was only a matter of time until they fed the alcohol to the cheese, and the cheese to themselves. Chimay takes its name from the beer it's washed in—Chimay—which nurtures the cheese into a semisoft state: pungent, full-flavored, and meaty, without the petrol sharpness that can develop in French washed rinds. Don't rub your hands all over it, lest you alienate your friends; rest assured, however, that the flavor is mellow and bacony. Get a big bottle of Chimay and settle in for a religious experience.

COBB HILL ASCUTNEY MOUNTAIN

USA | RAW | HARD | VEGETARIAN

Gail Holmes lives in the small community of Hartland Four Corners, Vermont, where neighbors tend Jersey cows that roam across grass fields and produce thick, organic milk. The best raw material for good cheese goes into this New England take on an Alpine recipe. Ten months of aging produces a wheel that's best in the winter, when the nutty, sweet, moderately sharp flavor is most suitable. It's almost toasty, like pignoli in a hot skillet. A hint of roasted hazelnuts and chestnuts adds to the wintry character. A slightly sweet, Belgian-style brew with warm gingerbread undertones is the ticket. Here in New York, we like Hennepin.

COBB HILL FOUR CORNERS CAERPHILLY

USA | RAW | FIRM | VEGETARIAN

The flip side to the American original **Ascutney Mountain** is this Vermont take on the classic Welsh miner's cheese, **Caerphilly**. Certified organic milk makes this **Cheddar** variant an unusual success, better than many we've had from Wales! A dusty, brushed rind encases a firm, flaking paste of a lovely pale yellow. Pronounced buttermilk tang balances a crumbly wedge. Satisfying with a clean, citrusy *weitbier* (go find Hoegaarden).

COMTÉ (GRUYÈRE DE COMTÉ) 🐄

FRANCE | RAW | FIRM | A.O.C.

One of the world's greatest cheeses, this fine specimen of small cooperative cheesemaking is from the Jura in eastern Franche-Comté. More Comté is made than any other French cheese and it's no wonder, considering a single wheel weighs about ninety pounds (that's 140 gallons of milk!). Small herds graze throughout the summer on Alpine grass, their milk is pooled, and Comté is made in mountain huts; it's aged for many months, sometimes up to two years, before it sees a market. Like Swiss **Gruyère**, the firm, supple paste has aromas of cooked milk, butter, and hazelnuts, and is dotted with olive-pit-sized "eyes," or holes. The flavor is supremely balanced and fruity, though sweeter and mellower than that of its Swiss cousins. Melted, it adds depth and roundness to traditional fondue, and softens the edge on rustic Rhône reds.

CONE DU PORT AUBRY 🐐

FRANCE | RAW | FRESH

This raw goat's milk cheese has it all—depth of flavor and a great story. In a moment of desperation, when its maker had run out of **Crottin de Chavignol** molds and was searching frantically for a receptacle for his fresh curd, a solution presented itself: his wife's brassiere, hanging on a clothesline. Thank goodness for Madame's generous breast; the resulting two-pound, Hershey Kiss–shaped wedge has all the lip-smacking density of good **Pouligny-Saint Pierre**: moist, tangy, delicately vegetal. The C-size mound of fluffy, goaty cake is happily married with Loire Valley Sauvignon Blanc of the Sancerre persuasion.

CONSIDER BARDWELL FARM METTOWEE 🐐

USA | PASTEURIZED | FRESH | VEGETARIAN

People tend to think of goat cheese as white and spreadable, a bit tangy, something akin to cream cheese. But good goat cheese is so much more. It's zesty but not abrasive, with a pristine softness and flavor of lemon. That's Mettowee, from West Pawlet, Vermont. There's no rind or ash. It's "just" impeccably fresh goat cheese, without a trace of the grit you're sometimes unlucky enough to find in this type. Find it in the Northeast, from April to January, and when you do, go New Zealand Sauvignon Blanc for some lush tropical fruit flavors with your goat.

COOLEA 🐄

IRELAND | PASTEURIZED | HARD

Dutch immigrants Dick and Helene Willems found a lovely swath of countryside in Coolea, county Cork, and decided to look to their roots for cheese-making inspiration. They began producing their signature Coolea, a Dutch **Gouda**-style cheese, in the eighties, and their son Dickie is now overseeing the curds. The resulting paste is deep buttercup-yellow, with a satisfyingly chewy texture. As with all good aged Goudas, look for long, lingering flavors of whiskey, toast, and caramel. Coolea is especially sweet and rich, one of a few that can sit alongside a big, juicy California Zinfandel or heady, spicy Aussie Shiraz.

COWGIRL CREAMERY MT. TAM

USA | PASTEURIZED | BLOOMY | VEGETARIAN

The cowgirls, Sue Connelly and Peg Smith, don't wrangle cattle. They milk 'em. Well, actually, they don't milk 'em. They buy milk from the highly esteemed, certified organic, family-owned Straus Family Creamery near Point Reyes Station, California, where cowgirls and cowboys tend this happy herd of Holstein and Jersey cows. Sue and Peg know the best milk makes the best cheese. Mt. Tam, which we like on delicate fennel crackers, resembles a mottled white hockey puck. Beneath its thick skin, this fluffy triple-crème has pronounced aromas of mushroom and wet straw. Give the cheese a few weeks to mature, when the inside is so melting, you might dig it out with your fingers (while the guests aren't looking). When eating a cheese that's like thick, beaten butter, our golden rule is to cut the fat with effervescence: soft Moscato d'Asti or California sparklers.

COWGIRL CREAMERY RED HAWK

USA | PASTEURIZED | WASHED RIND | VEGETARIAN

This is the only instance in the entire world (that we know of) where a cheesemaker has created a triple-crème washed-rind. The cowgirls combined 75 percent butterfat and beefy, brined, full-on flavor. Everyone who tastes this diminutive wheel goes ga-ga. The cheese, made from certified organic milk from the Straus Family Creamery, is as rich and weightless as good face cream, and all that fat carries bacony, winey, seemingly endless flavor. Eat the rind, suck your fork, bang the table. Voted Best Cheese in America in 2003, it's sure to be one of the best for years to come. Lighten the fatty, stinky punch with a crisp, aromatic wine, like West Coast Fumé Blanc.

CRAVANZINA

ITALY | PASTEURIZED | BLOOMY

Piedmont produces a great array of runny, bloomy, buttery beauties that actually make it to the U.S. export market. A mix of sheep's and cow's milk, they are small and meant to be eaten when relatively young. This thin, oozing patty is only one example. Pasteurization renders the flavor quite mild, but there is an abundant range of gentle grass, milk, and cream. A great starter cheese, and a true crowd-pleaser. Something a little floral, a little spritzy, like a Moscato d'Asti, would be right.

CRAVE BROTHERS LES FRERES

USA | PASTEURIZED | WASHED RIND

The four Crave Brothers created this luscious, pudgy round to reflect their Irish-French heritage, and sure enough it reminds us of a cross between **Ardrahan** and Pont-l'Evêque. A semisoft cheese that leaves a hint of stink on your fingertips, the main impression is of damp smoke and bacony depths. A woody, tobacco-laden mouthful of Oregon Pinot Noir complements the masculine heft.

CREMEUX DE BOURGOGNE

FRANCE | PASTEURIZED | BLOOMY

Most of our fluffy, fatty triple-crèmes hail from northern Ile-de-France. Not so here. From the Beaune in Burgundy, Jacques Delin and his small group of fifteen employees hand mold each three-pounder of cream-enriched cow's milk. Originally crafted to be like **Brillat-Savarin,** with longer acidification and less rennet for a loose, softer paste, Cremeux now gets to the United States in excellent condition due to modifications in production. Meaning: more rennet, a firm set, and a cheese more like the industrial St. André and Explorateur. It's the best of the two predominant triple-crème styles: milky, sweet, with incredibly rich mousse and a thin skin of a rind. To drink, try something sparkling, or the rarified Pinot Noirs from Cremeux's land of production.

CRESCENZA

See **Stracchino**

CROTTIN

FRANCE | RAW/PASTEURIZED | FRESH

Fresh and rindless, Crottin is made for immediate consumption. Often sliced and baked to garnish a salad, like the best fresh goat cheeses, these little guys smack of bright, lemony acidity and rich, clean milk. Enliven the green grass flavors with a fruity South African white.

CROTTIN DE CHAVIGNOL

FRANCE | RAW | FRESH | A.O.C.

Real Crottin de Chavignol must be made of raw milk, though you're likely to see the pasteurized imitation "Crottin Champcol" marketed under this sacred name, which literally means "turd." Crottin ages into fossilized, crusty rounds that develop a blanket of dark blue mold. Rustic, tangy, and piquant, it will make your mouth water for hours. Neighboring Sancerre or other Loire Sauvignon Blancs are the ticket for any picnic.

CROZIER BLUE

IRELAND | PASTEURIZED | BLUE | VEGETARIAN

The Grubbs perfected their signature Irish blue, **Cashel**, and then branched out and made a blue with sass. With a flock of East Friesian sheep that graze around the Rock of Cashel in county Tipperary, the Grubbs produce a spicy, verdant blue that can comfortably hold its own against **Roquefort**. Fatty sheep milk is the ideal vehicle for a blue that's bold and peppery. If Cashel Blue likes a sweet wine with a bit of toasty oxidation, Crozier does better with a sweet, floral number to placate its power. We like a late-harvest Riesling.

CYPRESS GROVE HUMBOLDT FOG

USA | PASTEURIZED | BLOOMY | VEGETARIAN

Humboldt County, California, is known for three things: growing more weed than anywhere else in the United States, the ubiquitous fog, and the immaculate cheese Humboldt Fog. Pioneering cheesemaker Mary Keehn has created an American classic, at once tangy and herbal, with two moist layers divided by a delicate line of ash, and a crumbly, lactic tang that is perfection. A perfect layer cake of a cheese, it's one of Murray's best sellers. We like it best for dessert with a round, juicy Riesling from California or Washington.

CYPRESS GROVE MIDNIGHT MOON

HOLLAND | PASTEURIZED | HARD

From the award-winning line of cheeses known as Creamline, overseen by cheesemaking pioneer Mary Keehn, here is the embodiment of aged goat **Gouda**. The best way to make a good Gouda is to get some help from the Dutch, and lo, this cheese is in fact produced in Holland. The selection and maturation specifications come from years of experience making American classics such as **Humboldt Fog**. Here is its flavor-intense counterpart. The bone-white paste is dense but creamy, with an incredibly long, sweet, caramelized finish. Its mildness belies its nutty complexity, reminiscent of butterscotch or toffee. Midnight Moon is brilliant alongside the insistent fruit of a California Cabernet, produced near Mary's McKinleyville farm.

DÉLICE DE BOURGOGNE

FRANCE | PASTEURIZED | BLOOMY

Unlike most French bloomies, which hail from Ile-de-France, this thick, frosted specimen is from

Burgundy, and its complexity belies its industrial production. Going beyond gut-busting richness, this triple-crème has a pungent, moldy rind with straw and mushroom aromas to complement the sweet, creamy, straw-colored interior. Delice rivals other bloomy rinds with its voluptuous, mouth-coating texture and its salty, earthy finish. The thick, dusty rind is a tricky pair: A regional approach would suggest a white Burgundy, so drink Chardonnay, but go easy on the oak.

DÉLICE DE SAINT-CYR

FRANCE | RAW | BLOOMY

While most triple-crèmes are enrobed in an elegant, stark-white mold, Délice de Saint-Cyr is a tiny treat of pale buttercup with little distinction between the rind and paste. Enriched with cream, it's rich and luscious, with the texture of whipped butter. Delicate, it dissolves into wisps of nothingness on the tongue. The flavor is sturdier than that of most triple-crèmes—leathery, with a peppery finish. Thus, it's better suited to flowery Grüner Veltliner than to Champagne.

DOUBLE GLOUCESTER

ENGLAND | RAW/PASTEURIZED | FIRM

Many know Double Gloucester, from the county of Gloucester, as the neon-orange layer wedged against **Stilton** to make Huntsman. Others know it from the two-hundred-year-old race in Gloucestershire, where hundreds of daredevils chase an eight-pound wheel of this cheese to the bottom of a heart-stoppingly steep hill. The versions worth eating are cloth wrapped, made from raw milk, and taste like sherbety **Cheddar**; we suggest the ones from the ladies—Mrs. Appleby and Mrs. Quicke. What makes it "double"? The whole milk from the morning and evening milkings are combined to make a richer variety than the "single," which mixes the skimmed product of the twice-daily milkings. In the United States, it is rare to find the latter. Traditionally colored with carrot juice or saffron, these days it's the vegetable dye annatto that imparts a sunny hue. Soft, mellow, buttery flavor accompanies the firm, crumbly texture. It is an ideal partner for bold accompaniments. So put together your own version of the classic English ploughman's lunch with pickled onions and chutney, washed down with a rich, nut-brown ale, like Newcastle.

DRUNKEN GOAT (QUESO DE MURCIA AL VINO)

SPAIN | PASTEURIZED | SEMISOFT | D.O.

The literal translation "washed with wine" says it perfectly. Maybe the cheesemakers were sitting around Murcia one day, sipping wine in the hot sun, when some drunkard knocked the cheese into a nearby barrel. Who knows? In any event, the result was so popular that they're making it on purpose these days. Semisoft, slightly aged goat cheese is cured for two to four days in local Yecla or Jumilla red wine: The paste remains white, while the violet rind imparts a fresh, fruity grapiness that is mild, sweet, and easy to eat, with no hint of animal. An easy, crowd-pleasing introduction to the family of wine-soaked cheeses often known (at least to Italians) as *ubriaco*. Drunken goats don't require anything serious; a savory strawberry Crianza Rioja does just fine.

DURRUS

IRELAND | RAW | WASHED RIND

Jeffa Gill is another of the Irishwomen responsible for the resurrection of that country's farmhouse cheese production. Produced in county Cork, Jeffa's cheese is made with raw milk. While Durrus is similar in style and origin to **Ardrahan** and **Gubbeen**, we find that raw milk makes a distinct difference. Approachable but complex, the compact paste is punctuated with tiny airholes, and though yielding, the paste is never runny. Its flavor tends more to the tomme styles than to washed-rinds: fruity but vegetal, with the heady smells of musty cellar and wet earth. The rind tends to be somewhat thick and gritty, so we like to trim it before eating. Those moist cave aromas balance with many wines, especially whites with residual sweetness. Try Vouvray or Auslese Riesling.

EL SUSPIRO (TORTA DE LOS MONTES DE TOLEDO)

SPAIN | PASTEURIZED | SEMISOFT

Produced in southern Spain, adjacent to the home of another famed goat cheese, **Ibores**, this saucer of a wheel has been made for little more than a decade. The scaly, elephant-gray rind may crack and bulge in its effort to contain the succulent, semisoft paste, which, when perfectly ripe, can be scooped like **Torta del Casar**. With a flavor somewhere between acidic and sour and a persistent, buttery finish, this relative newcomer pairs well with whites that have seen some wood. We especially like white Rioja.

EMMENTHALER

SWITZERLAND | RAW | FIRM

From the valley of the Emme River in the Alpine hills of central Switzerland to the corner deli, there are Emmenthalers aplenty. Be aware of the quality you are getting (or not): If it has no rind, looks like plastic, and has red stamping along its spine, stay far away. The one you want began its life as an enormous, bulging, 180-pound wheel, punctuated by gaseous "Swiss cheese holes" as big as a kid's fist. It was aged in a cave beneath the canton of Lucerne, and the smudgy, dark brown rind is a dead giveaway, as are the complex flavors not found in factory varieties. This is the real Swiss, with a pronounced fruitiness like condensed milk and a nip on the finish. A necessary one-third of any fondue, along with **Appenzeller** and **Gruyère**, this cheese is the classic melter of all time. The rich berry of California Zinfandel can handle Emmenthaler's unusual sweetness; if you're making fondue, stick with tradition and break open the Riesling.

EPOISSES DE BOURGOGNE

FRANCE | RAW/PASTEURIZED | WASHED RIND | A.O.C.

This is the classic washed-rind stinker you've read about in the tabloids; it's rumored to be banned from public transportation in France due to its powerful aroma. Although its history dates back to the sixteenth century, Epoisses de Bourgogne became endangered and all but disappeared in the early to mid-1900s, due to the loss of nearly half of France's population during World Wars I and II. It wasn't until the mid-1950s that M. Berthaut resumed production of this beloved cheese. The best versions are raw milk, but you'll find them only in Europe. Here in the States, look for the often puddlelike, pasteurized version in the little wooden box. Its orange smear-rind develops with weekly washings in brandylike Marc de Bourgogne. Salty and runny, with a mild bite, Epoisses is best when it's ripe enough to dunk your bread in the luscious, succulent ooze. Your choices of wine are versatile, from Alsatian Riesling to California Cabernet.

ERBORINATO DI PECORA

ITALY | RAW | BLUE

Looking for a subtle blue for your next dinner party? Then this is not the cheese for you. Italy thumbs its nose at **Roquefort** with this huge, bold, peppery, verdant blue that practically explodes in your mouth; it's been burning tongues since the time of the ancient Romans. The challenging if impeccable balance of salt, spice, and creaminess is not to be missed. The often brown pallor can be a bit off-putting, but don't be deterred. The viscous syrup of white dessert wines like Muscat, from France to California, soothes the sharp edges.

EVORA

PORTUGAL | RAW | FIRM | VEGETARIAN | D.O.P.

Another wild offering from the Portuguese down in Biera: a waxen puck smelling of damp pasture and lanolin. Rustic, to be sure, it fairly reeks of yeast, and the little nubbins of rind that lodge in your teeth are piquant and vegetal. When properly ripe, expect whipped, bulging insides that are sweet and fatty. Years ago, small rounds of Evora were used instead of coins to pay workers. We prefer money, but a chunk of this and a slice of chorizo on a summer picnic will do us just fine. For the wine, try the bracing white Vinho Verde.

FETA, BULGARIAN

BULGARIA | PASTEURIZED | FRESH

You haven't tried feta until you've tried Bulgaria's take. If **French feta** is delicate, creamy, and balanced, Bulgarian feta will beat you up and steal your car. Aggressively salty, the extraordinary, crumbly paste tastes of oil-cured Moroccan olives. Cut the salt with sautéed spinach in spanokopita, and enjoy the deep, marinated flavors unique to this version of feta. You might think a tough cheese like this needs a domineering drink to slap it into submission, but we recommend a light, citrusy wheat beer to offset that salt.

FETA, FRENCH OR

FRANCE | PASTEURIZED | FRESH

Leave it to the French to corner the feta market in a couple of decades. Although France has been producing feta for only twenty-five years, the United States imports more from that upstart than from Greece, Bulgaria, and all the Balkans combined. French feta began as an ingenious use of excess sheep milk from the region of **Roquefort**, where a huge producer, Lactalis, needed to make a new cheese to avoid flooding the Roquefort market with too much blue. Today there are goat as well as sheep versions. Known for a milder, less salty flavor than its counterparts, French feta is aged in salted whey, not just brine, for lip-smacking creaminess. Crumble it atop a cucumber, tomato, and red onion salad, and pour your pals a glass of rosé while relaxing on the patio.

FETA, GREEK

GREECE | PASTEURIZED | FRESH

The original is often the best, and in this case, famed Greek feta is pretty unbeatable—milder than Bulgarian, more complex than French. The sheep's milk delivers a round fattiness in the mouth that offsets the bright tanginess and salt of the brine in which it stews. It's another one for cooking—crumbled in omelets, mixed into summer salads. Clean, milky, saline, consistent. When in doubt, choose the original. For authenticity, pour some retsina into your glass.

FIORE SARDO

ITALY | RAW/PASTEURIZED | FIRM | D.O.P.

This "Sardinian Flower" is not the delicate shrinking violet you might expect. Traditional raw milk versions produced in mountain huts called *pinnette* are smoked over open fires and rubbed down with olive oil and sheep fat to encourage ripening. More commercial pasteurized versions are made without the smoke and the lard. In each instance the craggy, flaking paste is *rustico*: You feel the fat of the sheep milk, and the taste is savory, with grassy flavors more like bark and wood than fresh spring herbs. Rustic cheese calls for rustic wine: Sangiovese, as in Chianti, rough tannins be damned; this flower will mow 'em down.

FISCALINI BANDAGED CHEDDAR

USA | RAW | FIRM | VEGETARIAN

A unique American Cheddar from cheesemaker Jorge "Mariano" Gonzales. Made in Modesto, California, this one is firm, balanced, and sharp without being bitter—thank the cheesecloth for that. The American Cheese Society has recognized the eighteen-month version as the best farmstead cheese in America, while the thirty-month took a silver medal at the World Cheese Awards. One of the few Cheddars we've found on U.S. soil that approaches the perfect balance of lean almond and dried grass in the true English farmhouse versions. A California Cabernet keeps it local and harmonious.

FISCALINI SAN JOAQUIN GOLD

USA | RAW | FIRM | VEGETARIAN

Back at the World Cheese Awards, this Gold scored gold in 2004. We guess it's because of the marriage between firm grate-ability and a mellow sweetness absent from most farmhouse **Cheddars**. It's like Cheddar the way some wish it might be: hearty, less acidic, with an aroma of toasted nuts and browned butter. Incredibly versatile, from indulgent grilled cheese to vegetable gratin, it pairs nicely with a thick, dark beer, like Guinness.

FLEUR DU MAQUIS

FRANCE | RAW/PASTEURIZED | SEMISOFT

Similar to another well-known Corsican—**Brin d'Amour**—Fleur du Maquis is named for the wildflowers growing across the island. With age the rind, crusted with herbs such as rosemary and sariette, develops into a frightening, furry mass that remains edible, though the potency of dried herbs is biting. Strongly perfumed with hot, sunny maquis underbrush, the fine, ivory paste is slightly salty, sour, and very sexy. Grab a bottle of spicy red Côtes du Rhône.

FONTINA D'AOSTA

ITALY | RAW | WASHED RIND | D.O.P.

We all know Fontina that comes conveniently packaged in neat Cryovac squares in the grocer's dairy case, often decorated with a red plastic rind, and probably made in Wisconsin. *This* is not that Fontina (or more accurately, that's not Fontina at all). This name-protected version, with a pedigree extending back to the 1200s, is made from the milk of Alpine-grazing cows. The burnished, crusty rind develops after washing and brushing, protecting a pale-golden interior riddled with small holes. The flavor is rich and nutty, reminiscent of truffle and roasted apple, with a supple texture that's extraordinarily meltable. A central ingredient in Piedmont's famed *fondutta*, similar to Swiss fondue, this Fontina is blended to orgiastic rapture with cream, eggs, and shaved white truffle. Regional wisdom recommends you grab a glass of Barbaresco or other Nebbiolo-based wine.

FÖRSTERKÄSE

SWITZERLAND | RAW | WASHED RIND

Försterkäse means "lumberjack cheese," a name that implies big, burly, woolly rusticity. In fact, the cheese is groan-inducingly good, produced by a single dairy run by two second-generation cheesemakers. Maturation is overseen by Swiss *affineur* Rolf Beeler. One of the most exceptional cheeses in the world, made in Switzerland's rolling, orchard-dotted landscape of Toggenburg, northeast of Zurich, Försterkäse takes its name from the bark band encircling the thick, oozing paste. Though the cheese is brine washed, the flavor remains sweet and milky, with heady pine and sap aromas. We tend not to drink or speak while consuming as much Försterkäse as possible, but a glass of white Côtes du Rhône will drag out the experience delightfully.

FOUGERUS

FRANCE | RAW/PASTEURIZED | BLOOMY

Sitting stout and pretty, this grande dame looks like a small, double-stacked wheel of **Brie** with a decorative fern on top. What it lacks in surface area it makes up for in complexity: The aroma of forest floor melds with the mushroom and slight ammonia scent of the rind, deepening what would otherwise be a straightforward, sweet, salty, lactic paste. She's a delicate one, prone to overripeness. By the time the paste is creamy throughout, the rind tends toward heavy ammonia. When in doubt, select a piece still chalky inside but spreadable on dainty water crackers. Savor with a glass of round, white Bordeaux.

FOURME D'AMBERT

FRANCE | RAW/PASTEURIZED | BLUE

Even self-professed haters of blue fall for this gentle, voluptuous, curdy beaut. Critics call it Saga for grown-ups, but the good stuff is miraculous: rich, thick, liberally pocked cylinders of blue beneath a smooth, firm rind smelling of cave. Milky yet complex, leathery and earthy, it has none of the fierce residual pepper of better-known **Roquefort**. Go light and sweet, with thin slices of pear and a tawny port.

FROMAGE D'AFFINOIS

FRANCE | PASTEURIZED | BLOOMY

Anyone who has spent any amount of time behind Murray's cheese counter has doubtless encountered customers mistaking Fromage d'Affinois for **Brie**. Just because it's made in France, from cow's milk, soft-ripened, and covered with a soft, bloomy rind, does this mean it's Brie? No, Fromage d'Affinois is its own cheese, produced from milk that has been specially filtered to yield a silkier texture than that of Brie. Its sweet, mild flavor precludes the mushroomy earthiness normally found in its identical-looking cousin. Accentuate the lusciousness with a glass of fresh-berry Beaujolais.

Fromage de Meaux

See **Brie**

GABIETOU

FRANCE | RAW | FIRM

A new find on the Murray's counter, this Pyrénées mixed-milk encapsulates the greatness of mountain cheese: a happy marriage between the bold fruitiness of Swiss cheeses and the restrained, elegant grassiness of **Ossau-Iraty** types from the French Pyrénées. These smaller wheels (eight pounds or so) age more quickly than Ossau-Iraty, but the paste remains unctuous and fatty. On first bite, you think benign, mild, and then there is the flavor pop: layers of salt, aromatic spice, toasted nut, and the first whisper of butterscotch. Expect a few minutes to pass before the residual sharpness dies down, tempered by a glass of juicy cherry, as in Beaujolais.

GAMONEDO (QUESO GAMONEDO)

SPAIN | RAW | BLUE | D.O.

Like its Asturian cousin **Cabrales**, Gamonedo was originally made with the milk of mixed herds shepherded into the Picos de Europa with the coming of spring. Scrappy, scavenging goats and sheep were sent up the hillsides to clear paths for lumbering herds of cattle requiring ample grass. Wheels aged in small mountain huts absorbed the aromatic smoke of open fires maintained for warmth. Today, Gamonedo is largely made from cow's milk, but retains its remote, rustic flavors. The dry, sandy paste develops blue mold naturally when cut, its rough rind falling away in flakes. Tart and smoky, the flavor is reminiscent of a piquant blue but doesn't pack the punch of Cabrales. Sip an Oloroso sherry to play up the smoky, toasted soul of this rare treasure.

GAPERON

FRANCE | RAW/PASTEURIZED | SEMISOFT

Traditionally, these soft, fat globes were hung outside homes in France's central Auvergne as an indication of prosperity and used as dowries during marriage arrangements. Freshly skimmed milk was added to the milk from the butter churn before curing by an open fire. The final ball was wrapped in decorative yellow ribbon. These days we love it because it is naturally low in fat, with a flavor enhanced by black pepper and garlic. Think of it as high-end Boursin, or "the salami of cheese." Pudgy, with intense aromas of earth, this is perfectly paired with Merlot and a hunk of sausage.

GARROTXA (QUESO DE LA GARROTXA)

SPAIN | PASTEURIZED | SEMISOFT

The *txa* is Catalan and is pronounced *cha*. It's *Ga-RO-cha*, and well worth knowing. With its traditional moldy-gray, fuzzy rind, this aged wheel is a brilliant expression of goat's milk at its best. The wheels remain cakey, with the woodsy flavor of pine nuts. Produced in northeast Spain (Catalonia), the cheese has inspired imposters across Spain who have hopped on the Garrotxa bandwagon, prompting the application for a new D.O. to protect a local specialty. Our producer of choice knows his limits: He sold his goats to the neighbor and buys the milk back to produce and age this cheese in his backyard facility. The rind is best left uneaten. Superb with Catalan Cava or whites from Rías Baixas.

GJETOST

NORWAY | PASTEURIZED | HARD

An amazing if somewhat revolting cheese, Gjetost is made from the whey of goat's and cow's milk. But up in Norway, they love it; it's their PowerBar. Each block resembles stiff peanut butter, with that deep tan color, but the texture is positively waxen. The flavor bears no resemblance to cheese, but is sweet and caramelized, not unlike fudge. Tuck some into your snowsuit for the next time you're lost in the woods. And to stay warm in the cold, grab a bottle that's generous with the fruit (and the alcohol)—a California Zinfandel, for example.

GORGONZOLA

ITALY | PASTEURIZED | BLUE | D.O.P.

The fact that this is one of the first blue cheeses to develop a following in the United States, where consumers ask for it by name, means there are excellent versions of Gorgonzola as well as precut, foil-wrapped wedges. Quality Gorgonzola is produced in Piedmont and Lombardy, in wheels that weigh up to twenty-six pounds, depending on the style. The two milder, creamier versions are *dolce* and *cremificato*. The difference between them? The former is so mild it's bland, and produced for export to the American market. The so-called *cremificato* has a higher water content and is preferred by Italians. The lumpy, luscious, scoopable paste can develop some serious pungency after two months of maturation. So wet is the cheese that when pierced, to begin the process of blueing, the tunnels simply collapse onto themselves, preventing aggressive molding. You're more apt to notice small pockmarks of blue, but little veining.

The mountain, or *piccante*, style is firmer and drier, with bright blue striations of mold. More mold means a peppery, spicy flavor. Some wheels may be aged as long as three hundred days, by which time they are sandy, gray-brown, and eye-wateringly fierce.

Turn to Italy's famed Moscato d'Asti, or a variant made with pears rather than grapes, for sweet companionship.

GOUDA

HOLLAND | RAW/PASTEURIZED | HARD

As farmhouse **Cheddar** is to England, Gouda is to Holland. We speak not of supermarket Gouda, with its red plastic wax coating like penny-candy lips. That version is mass-produced, usually processed, gummy, and tart. Treat yourself to the glorious sweetness of real aged Gouda and you will never go back.

These smaller-production cheeses are aged, typically for at least one year, and many are made with unpasteurized milk, such as the group of cheeses known as **Boerenkaas**. *Boer* means "farmer" and *kaas* means "cheese," and as you may have guessed, they are farmstead produced. Seek out larger wheels, about twenty to thirty pounds. They will likely be covered in straw-yellow or chestnut-brown wax. With age, these wheels become dry and crunchy, with intense, layered, burnt-sugar-caramel-butterscotch flavor.

Only raw milk, small-production wheels qualify as Boerenkaas, but other aged Gouda types capture that rough sweetness and come by many brand names. The best-known younger variety is **Prima Donna**, and our new favorite aged Gouda, only eighteen to twenty-four months but somewhere in flavor between bourbon and toffee, is Beemster Classic. Rock-hard, flavor-dense **Roomano** is aged for only three years, but is made in smaller wheels that quickly develop candied intensity. While similar to an aged Gouda, it is technically from the cheese family Proosdy, which means that it has lower butterfat (45 percent) than the 48 percent required for Gouda. The wheel's edges are noticeably sharper, nearly squared off. Production is still quite small: The single manufacturer makes six hundred to eight hundred wheels every three weeks.

GOAT GOUDA

HOLLAND | PASTEURIZED | HARD

Younger goat gouda, aged for several months, has a mild, supple, chalk-white paste with vague sweetness and pleasant, if relatively innocuous, character. The aged versions become rough and stony, with a dense, toffee-colored interior dotted with generous white patches. Don't be fooled: They are not salt, but rather tyrosine (amino acid) clusters that result from long and patient aging. They also lend that addictive crunch. The youthful suggestion of sweetness intensifies into a caramelized, burnt-sugary treasure.

Both cow and goat versions of **Boerenkaas** and Gouda find ample partnership with New World superfruity, high-alcohol reds such as California Cabernet or Australian Shiraz. Get loopy tonight.

GRAFTON FOUR STAR CHEDDAR

USA | RAW | FIRM | VEGETARIAN

The Grafton Village Cheese Company in southern Vermont, perhaps the leading Cheddar producer in America, makes a variety of aged and flavored Cheddars from local Jersey cow's milk, the hallmark of Vermont Cheddar. Rindless, satisfying, and crumbly, they are ideal for snacking or cooking as the cheesy molten center of a morning omelet. Although there are five and six-year-old versions, we bank on the forty-eight month Four Star. It's got plenty of bite without searing your throat. An amber lager, football, and a crowd pair well.

GRANA PADANO

ITALY | RAW | HARD | D.O.P.

It must have been one of those "Eureka!" moments. In the twelfth century, Benedictine and Cistercian monks, who had cleared the Paduan plain for agriculture, came upon a solution for extending the shelf life of the abundant milk of their cattle: hard cheese. Soft cheeses, made from simply curdling milk, were already prevalent, but they were still too perishable. The monks took things a step further when they removed the whey from the curds. The result was a dense cheese that could last indefinitely, and this type became known as *grana* (grain) because of its granular texture. Centuries later, many know Grana Padano as the pale imitation of superstar **Parmigiano-Reggiano** (produced farther north throughout the Po River Valley) and unfortunately write it off. What a shame, because this straw-yellow wheel, made from partially skimmed milk and aged for twelve to thirty-six months, is fragrant and delicate, with a marked, sweet toastiness. Sure, you can grate it or shred it over an arugula salad. But give this cheese a chance to shine with Parma's classic partner—dry, effervescent Lambrusco—and you'll understand that naturally low fat is a beautiful thing.

GRAZALEMA (QUESO DE GRAZALEMA)

SPAIN | RAW/PASTEURIZED | FIRM

A plasticky yellow, honeycombed rind doesn't promise much, but Grazalema is a wolf in sheep's clothing. Firm, fatty, and melting, and the low acidity means you get deep, citrus flavor without the bite of aged **Manchego**. The hot, sunny, southern Spanish province of Cádiz coaxes sweet, ripe pear and nectarine notes that remind us of chocolate-dipped fruit. The rich, succulent paste melts in the mouth and is best with a buttery Chardonnay, like so many made in California.

GREAT HILL BLUE

USA | RAW | BLUE

Nearly a hundred years tending Jersey and Holstein cows is bound to teach you something about fresh milk. Tim Stone's family has been in just that situation, and now as head cheesemaker on the family farm in Marion, Massachusetts, Tim produces a kicking blue with milk straight from the udder—unhomogenized and thick with butterfat. For the cheese eater that means a deep-yellow paste mottled with bright blue veining that is dense and creamy with spicy, mouthwatering flavor. Great Hill is a robust example of the predominant style in American blues, rindless and full-on, but the roundness of fresh milk is what lingers on the palate, waiting to be complemented by a honeyed white wine like Gewürztraminer Spätlese.

GRUYÈRE

SWITZERLAND | RAW | FIRM

We beseech you: Just because you can find plasticky blocks of deli-slicing Gruyère does not mean you should eat them, especially when the true cave-aged wheels are nearly as ubiquitous. Dating back to at least the thirteenth century, Gruyère has been central to the history, culture, and trade of Switzerland's Fribourg canton, a region that was a crossroads for Celts, Helvetians, and Romans; the latter brought their cheesemaking expertise to the area. These days, following age-old tradition, enormous eighty-pound wheels (requiring eighty-eight gallons of milk *per wheel*) are produced by Swiss cooperatives throughout the Jura Mountains and cave aged for six to thirty-six months. Salty, nutty, almost beefy, the little crystalline bursts of flavor and crunch, interspersed throughout a solid, smooth paste, are the result of careful aging. One of the classic Alpine melters, Gruyère is what you've seen crusting your onion soup or oozing from your croque monsieur. Skip the soup and sandwich and melt it in a pot with **Appenzeller** and **Emmenthaler** for classic fondue.

This hefty mouthful is best suited to wintry evenings and big, rustic red wines from southern France, though we've also had ecstatic pairings with sweet sherry from the south of Spain.

GUBBEEN

IRELAND | PASTEURIZED | WASHED RIND | VEGETARIAN

The third of four great Irish washed-rind cheeses (with **Ardrahan**, **Durrus**, and **Milleens**), this beautiful offering is from Tom and Giana Ferguson of county Cork. It was inspired by both Giana's childhood in a family who revered *real* food and cheese, and the encouragement of Veronica Steele, originator of the first Irish farmstead cheese, Milleens. In an intoxicating display of *terroir*, lush, rolling hillsides feed the mixed herd of cows—including the rare and local black Kerry breed—and salty ocean air feeds the final flavors of this squishy tomme. The sticky, tan rind can be gritty to eat, but the buttery innards are deliciously complex: mushroom, salt, a bit of damp, packed earth. Eating Gubbeen is like catching a whiff of wood smoke on a wet, early spring day. Lighten it up with an off-dry, aromatic white like Vouvray.

HALLOUMI

CYPRUS | PASTEURIZED | FRESH

You may have seen Halloumi in the dairy case at Murray's, or perhaps at a market specializing in Middle Eastern foods. It's a rubbery little block, off-white and tightly wrapped in Cryovac, not usually what we'd associate with fine cheese. But there is a long and storied tradition here, and in the proper application, Halloumi is irreplaceable. Good versions are still made by hand throughout the Mediterranean island of Cyprus, shaped in straw containers, and stored in natural juices with salt water. The firm, salty, tangy paste has no rind and is used for cooking, sliced into slabs that are most often grilled and finished with oil, and perhaps pine nuts. The elastic paste holds its shape, never going gooey like most cheese, but developing a delicious golden crust that crunches before you hit that softened, tangy center. As part of this simple dish, a glass of something cool, crisp, and refreshing is best—say Pinot Grigio.

HARBOURNE BLUE

ENGLAND | PASTEURIZED | BLUE | VEGETARIAN

Here's your chance to find out what the only goat-milk blue in England tastes like. For twenty years, in Devon, Robin Congdon has produced this unusual combination. A blue cheese with minimal veining—what veins there are form a thin web of gray-green mold snaking across the fudgy, crumbly, white paste. The clean, salty, toasted nuttiness of good goat milk prevails, sure to please even the staunchest blue cheese hater. Maybe even the staunchest goat cheese hater. The dry, sweet paste is atypical for the type. Delicate dessert wines, like off-dry Vouvray, emphasize the brightness of the milk.

HOCH YBRIG

SWITZERLAND | RAW | FIRM

Bathe a cheese in white wine and you wind up with mellow, fruity sweetness. Bathe this **Gruyère**-style wheel—made by one dairy, of milk from the herds of several small farms—and you wind up with a symphony: a beautiful balance between gamy aroma and peppery spice, with layers of hazelnut and butterscotch on the finish. Hoch Ybrig offers up a rich brew of tastes best enjoyed during the cold winter months, although it's available year-round. The correct pronunciation is something like "hockey brig," named for the mountain immediately outside of Zurich. It was created in the 1980s in Ybergeregg—you're on your own pronouncing that one. This newcomer is sublime. Try it with a ripe, fruity wine; to bring notes of apricot to the foreground, we like Merlot.

IBORES (QUESO DE LOS IBORES)

SPAIN | RAW | FIRM | D.O.

On the stark, scalded plains of Spanish Extremadura, Verata and Retinta goats pick about nourishing the special milk that becomes Ibores. Some wheels are rubbed in smoky pimentón (paprika) and have a dry, oily paste. The wheels from producer Capribor, however, are smooth, caramel-colored revelations, with aromatics of sunbaked stone and toasted herbs. The complex flavor builds to an impressive, spicy crescendo. Here is the perfect picnic cheese with chorizo and sultry white Rioja.

IDIAZÁBAL (QUESO IDIAZÁBAL)

SPAIN | RAW | FIRM | D.O.

Chances are most respectable cheesemongers have heard worse attempts at pronouncing this one than you are about to make. It's *ee-dee-ah-THA-bahl*. Don't let your twisted tongue stop you from trying this rustic, gamy beauty from the wilds of the Basque country. It's hearty, oily, and immensely satisfying, with a flavor that smacks of rare lamb chops.

Originally hung in chimneys to drain, the wheels absorbed smoke of beech and hawthorn wood. These days, smoke rooms accomplish the aggressive campfire cure. On rare occasions you may find the meaty, unsmoked variety. Either way, make sure you serve it with a hearty red from Ribera del Duero or a Rioja that's got a few years on it.

INNES

ENGLAND | RAW | FRESH | VEGETARIAN

Joe Bennet makes this vegetarian farmstead delight from the unpasteurized milk of the large herd of goats living at Highlands Farm Dairy in Staffordshire. The freshest of the fresh, these buttons are made every day from two-hour-old milk for a soft, soufféd texture. Gentle and sweet with a subtle citruslike tang, this was the first cheese ever to twice be chosen as the Supreme

Champion at the British Cheese Awards. If you come across it in England, enjoy it with a rustic loaf of bread, a fresh green salad, and a bottle of crisp Sauvignon Blanc.

JASPER HILL ASPENHURST

USA | RAW | FIRM

There's not much to do in Vermont's Northeast Kingdom—might as well make excellent cheese. Greensboro's Kehler brothers produce this limited-edition farmstead sharpie using only the unpasteurized milk of their herd of Ayrshire cows. The mottled, gray-brown cloth rind is regularly brushed with melted lard during its nine-to-eighteen-month aging period. Don't be fooled by its **Cheddar**-like appearance; this cheese has not been cheddared—the process by which the curd has been cut into blocks and stacked. Rather, the blocks of curd are stirred at the bottom of the vat approximately every fifteen minutes until the desired acidity is reached. The difference between this and Cheddar making is a slower rate of acidification, resulting in a subtler, less aggressively sharp flavor. Aspenhurst is similar to a classic English Leicester: complex, nutty, and sweet, with a toffee finish. A perfect tablemate for a thick, dark beer, like Guinness.

JASPER HILL BARTLETT BLUE

USA | RAW | BLUE

A blue for those who don't like the blues, Bartlett is the sweeter of Jasper Hill's two blues, produced like **Aspenhurst** (though with the key addition of mold!) and aged for four to six months. Do not fear you are hallucinating, as the mold will grow and spread through the sweet, sturdy interior once the cheese is cut and exposed to air. It's a limited-edition cheese, so when you see it, get it, and serve it with a salad of fresh bitter greens and walnuts. Marry it with a glass of dry Madeira, a magical combination.

JASPER HILL BAYLEY HAZEN BLUE

USA | RAW | BLUE

Bayley-Hazen Road stretches for fifty-four miles in Vermont's Northeast Kingdom. Construction began during the Revolutionary War when some, including George Washington, thought Canada could easily be captured and made into the four-teenth colony. That idea was scrapped, and so was the building of the road. Fortunately for us, Jasper Hill Farm is continuing its cheesemaking endeavors, and the Kehler brothers have named their excellent blue for the historic road located in their neck of the woods. The delectable, firm paste is complex, tasting of sweet cream and nuts, with distinct licorice notes. From a state where many good cheeses are made, this one is exemplary. When serving Bayley Hazen Blue, put a big wedge on a board and chip away at it while you sip port and dream of tramping through the woods with Ethan Allen's Green Mountain Boys.

JASPER HILL CONSTANT BLISS

USA | RAW | BLOOMY

Picture this: It's a cool, damp Friday night in the cheese cave. A sexy little barrel of Ayrshire cow's-milk cheese has just come in, begging for attention. Lucky for her, hundreds of ambient molds are hanging out, waiting for the right girl. Mold meets cheese, rind becomes bloomy, happiness ensues. The result is a beautiful gray-and-white-mottled rind, mushroomy and vegetal, reeking of the cave where it all began. That damp, clay paste is the Kehlers' version of French **Chaource**, modified in shape and aging to last sixty days for legal sale. These little drums are named for a Revolutionary War scout rather than the state of being, but you will be in constant bliss with this cheese and a bottle of Champagne.

JASPER HILL WINNIMERE

USA | RAW | WASHED RIND

Named for the shore on Vermont's Caspian Lake where at least five generations of Kehlers have spent their summers, this is America's take on **Försterkäse**. Here's how it goes: Leave an open barrel of brew in the cave, let the yeasts take hold, and you've got a Lambic-style beer. And as those crafty (and admittedly drunken) Kehler boys tell it, feed the beer to the cheese.

After the cheese is made, it is washed in brine, bound in wood hoops chopped from the forest out back, and bathed in beer. The result: a soft, velvety paste with a hint of stink and Christmas tree. If you have been invited to a friend's lakeside home for a summer party, grab a bottle of Alsatian Gewürztraminer to accompany Winnimere, and get invited back.

JUNIPER GROVE TUMALO TOMME

USA | RAW | SEMISOFT

In Redmond, Oregon, Pierre Kolisch makes this elegant mountain-style wheel from the milk of Alpine, La Mancha, and Saanen breeds of goat. Each round is hand washed in a brine solution and aged on pine planks in a cellar cave for three to six months. The semifirm cheese displays a beautiful natural reddish-brown rind and fog-gray paste. Complex and nicely balanced, with a sweet full flavor that is pleasantly salty, Tumalo Tomme tastes of hazelnuts and hay, with a musty cellar finish. We recommend an Oregon Pinot Noir as a delicious accompaniment to this American original.

KAPITI KIKORANGI

NEW ZEALAND | PASTEURIZED | BLUE | VEGETARIAN

Kapiti Island lies on the Tasman Sea and is the namesake of New Zealand's Kapiti Cheese Company, makers of this creamy—nearly spreadable—blue, with deep moldy pockets in a golden-butter sea. The pale gray rind is often mottled with orange and red yeasty mold, with the distinct aroma of damp cellar to offset its mildly pungent kick and endnotes of wildflowers and butter. When you're that far away from the rest of the world, look to the neighboring Aussies for a good Cabernet.

KASSERI 🐄 OR 🐑

OR MIXED | GREECE | PASTEURIZED |
SEMISOFT

Like **Halloumi**, this is another Greek cheese that,
when used properly, is inimitable. It is used to
make Greece's famed saganaki, wherein the
cheese is sautéed in butter, sprinkled with lemon
juice, and occasionally set afire after a splash of
brandy. The smooth, **Provolone**-like paste is quite
sharp and salty, and, though firm, is creamy and
full in the mouth. Sure, you can grate it, but challenge yourself to branch out with your cheese,
and try slicing it into slabs for searing or grilling. It
makes an impressive summer lunch, with its
bright, olivey flavors, alongside a simple salad
and a glass of refreshing, juicy rosé.

LAGUIOLE 🐄

FRANCE | RAW | FIRM | A.O.C.

Laguiole's monastery origins date to the eleventh
century, according to local legend. The monks
taught the recipe to *buronniers*, whose descen-
dants still make the barrel-shaped cheese in
mountain huts, or *buron*. And like its Auvergne
brethren **Salers** and Cantal, Laguiole, from the
namesake village in the mountains of Aubrac,
France, is made by adding day-old curds to
fresh ones. After twenty-four or more hours, the
squeaky popcorn niblets have developed a deep
perfume and barny, sour flavor that determine the
final personality of this cheese six to nine months
later. It has a **Cheddary** texture, but without the
nuttiness you might expect. The town of Laguiole,

known for its fine knives, also produces the ideal wine accompaniment in full-throated Gigondas.

L'AMI DU CHAMBERTIN

FRANCE | RAW | WASHED RIND

The triumvirate of Burgundian washed-rind cheeses is completed by L'Ami du Chambertin: stronger than **Abbaye de Cîteaux**, but firmer and less intense than raw milk **Epoisses**. Washed in brine and Marc de Bourgogne, a spirit made from grape skins and twigs, L'Ami du Chambertin has the prickling aroma of fine, fruity brandy. Its glistening, quilted, orange rind covers a runny creamline, while the interior paste remains dense and clay-like. Definitely a room-clearer, but those who stick around to taste it are rewarded with a savory pudding: salty and milky, with a finish of fermented fruit. Pair regionally with a classic red Burgundy.

LANCASHIRE

ENGLAND | RAW/PASTEURIZED | FIRM

By now you've learned that if it's English, and high quality, there's likely a stoic farmwoman to thank. In this case, our preferred producer is Ruth Kirkham and her husband, John. Their farmstead Lancashire, made from the Kirkhams' herd of about forty Friesian cows, is brilliant for its subtle, crumbly, pale flesh. The firm, milky paste breaks in the mouth into chunks of clean, mellow curd with a heavenly tart finish. We think of it as **Cheddar** for summer, but the locals call it a "buttery crumble"— aptly named, since a few days after the cheeses are removed from their molds, then covered in cheesecloth in preparation for aging, Ruth rubs the dried barrels of cheese with a smooth layer of melted butter. Handle with care and drink responsibly—soft reds without abrasive tannins, like Italy's Barbaresco, have the right touch.

LANGRES

FRANCE | RAW/PASTEURIZED | WASHED RIND | A.O.C.

Barely legal, and we don't mean Girls Gone Wild, though they will, with a sliver of Langres after dinner. Unlike many beefy French stinkers, Langres has a spicy elegance to its dense, creamy paste. Brine washed and colored with roucou, a racy red coloring derived from the annatto tree, the squat cylinder is capped with an unusual concave top. A surprising shape until you learn that it's made in Champagne-Ardenne, where tradition dictates pouring a bit of local bubbly into the dip. A waterfall of yeasty effervescence rushes into the cut, heightening the fruit and pepper flavors. Since you're pouring Champagne, try to hit the flute, too.

LA SERENA (QUESO DE LA SERENA)

SPAIN | RAW | SEMISOFT | VEGETARIAN | D.O.

Deep in Extremadura, where Merino sheep forage on slate and granite soil, La Serena is testament to creative seasonal cheesemaking. Coagulated with cardoon thistle, this flabby saucer can be dangerous when ripe. It's so gooey you're liable to stick your thumb through the scaly brown crust and then be forced to eat the whipped, melting interior. For a party, carefully saw off the top and encourage guests to scoop the guts onto crusty bread. The thistle imparts an intense, vegetal, nearly sour flavor that's a beast to pair with wines. We like something faintly sweet but not overly floral, or a toasted, nutty Oloroso sherry.

LA TUR

ITALY | PASTEURIZED | BLOOMY

Three milks and two textures merge into one cheese's best approximation of ice cream. A thin, edible skin barely contains a hairbreadth of drippy tang, and then: deep, tongue-skimming, milk cloud, full and moist, with a liberal salting that makes you wish they left the sugar out of gelato entirely. A mild and delightful cheese. A little quaff of Prosecco and you might as well be dining in Piedmont.

LAVORT

FRANCE | RAW | FIRM

The land of the French Pyrénées abounds with legends of young shepherds discovering cheese after placing milk in a "canteen" made from an animal's stomach. This unusually shaped cheese from the central Auvergne has its own legend of a peasant named Guillaume who traveled across Europe during the Crusades, collecting inspiration and methods for the production of cheese. After inheriting land from his slain father figure, Baron Lavort, Guillaume swore to elevate the baron's name to greatness. He did so with a squat barrel of semi-aged cheese that resembled Auvergne's famous volcanoes, made with the pure milk of **Roquefort**'s Lacaune sheep. Aged from three to eight months on aromatic pine planks that impart a woody, fruity flavor, Lavort has a dense, toothsome texture and clean, sweet paste. Expect no gaminess. The delicate flintiness of whites such as Pouilly-Fumé offset the buttery richness.

LAZY LADY LA PETITE TOMME

USA | PASTEURIZED | BLOOMY

Vermont's Laini Fondiller is anything but a lazy lady; in fact, she's a goat-tending machine, though you'd never guess it by the gossamer-light touch of this little tomme, a thin, creamy, certified organic morsel cloaked in soft, earthy, blooming rind. After two weeks, Laini's tommes develop sandy mottling and a tang to offset their earthy mushroom notes. When the goats get lazy and their milk starts to wane toward fall, Laini adds a dash of cow's milk for her signature Demitasse. A straight Sauvignon Blanc is a bit harsh for these delicacies, so reach for the softer pear of Chenin Blanc in Vouvray or otherwise.

L'EDEL DE CLERON

FRANCE | PASTEURIZED | BLOOMY

Though you may have heard of the illustrious seasonal cheese **Vacherin Mont d'Or**, or been blessed enough to sneak a spoonful somewhere, it is very hard to find in America. L'Edel de Cleron, made in Franche-Comté by the producer Perrin, is probably the best-known "faux Vacherin" on the market. Available year-round, the cheese is made from milk that is gently pasteurized to retain maximum flavor, and the resulting cheese is bound with a strip of bark like the great Mont d'Or. It's a gently running, sweet, slightly woodsy cheese, and quite delicious. Do not compare it to the original, for it won't measure up; the fine, resinous smells and fatty, straw-fed milk won't be there. But if you settle in with a flute of Champagne and the expectation of a luscious, milky cheese, you'll be quite happy.

LE SARLET

FRANCE | PASTEURIZED | BLOOMY

This one is brand-new, from Poitou, and mighty fine it is, too. Hiding under the soft, tangy rind is a hint of ooze separating it from the thick, tender paste. The mild goat flavors are perfect for warm weather: light, bright, and refreshing. The voluptuous texture and even creaminess make it a crowd-pleaser, even more so with bracing Sancerre and/or a spoonful of linden honey.

LE VALLEROGER

FRANCE | RAW | WASHED RIND

During the winter, when industrial goat cheeses made with frozen curd are a bland, gummy mess, look for this rarity from one of only three producers in France's Rhône-Alpes. Washed in Seyssel, the local fruity white wine, this dinosaur egg ages for an unusually long time (as much as six months!), meaning its flavors are racy and raisiny, even in the dead of February. Some may say it's too crumbly, but that chalky core and peppery rind contrast beautifully. Dried cherries and light, soapy Soave make a high-low partnership.

LIMBURGER

USA | PASTEURIZED | WASHED RIND

One of the best known smelly cheese was originally beer washed in Belgian monasteries and named for the Limburg province, but Limburger's production in Germany became so prolific that the cheese is often considered to be of Bavarian origin. Most Americans know it as the inordinately smelly cheese of their youth, when it was made in Wisconsin to meet the great demand of the state's Germanic population. Today, there is a single producer left in Wisconsin, the Chalet Cheese Co-op. Small, half-pound blocks of this semisoft, incredibly stinky cheese can be found wrapped in foil. Avoid brown or slimy-looking pieces, if you're able to catch a glimpse before purchase. The flavor, once you get the cheese to your mouth, is actually quite mild, like salty, slightly fruity butter. This is a workingman's cheese, suitable for a slab of brown bread and a brewski, something straightforward like Sam Adams.

LINCOLNSHIRE POACHER

ENGLAND | RAW | FIRM

A little poaching in cheesemaking never hurts, especially if you take inspiration from the greats. Such is the case with brothers Simon and Tim Jones, who learned cheesemaking from the late Welshman Dougal Campbell, mountain climber and student of Swiss cheese producers, who arrived at the Joneses' farm with a bottle of rennet. The fourth-generation family dairy farm, located about ten miles from the sea, is one of the few in the area, and the Jones brothers take full advantage of what may seem like limitations specific to the region. The soil stratum is somewhat thin, with a chalky layer just beneath it, so the foliage is sparse and the terrain arid. However, the grasses have a unique complexity of flavor, thanks to the chalk, and it comes through in the milk.

The drier Lincolnshire summers result in decreased milk production, so this cheese is made only in the winter, when the cows are better fed and their milk naturally contains a higher fat content. Thus, what may seem like adversity actually produces a remarkable cheese. The waxy, pale blond paste looks like a **Cheddar** without the cloth binding, but the flavor is reminiscent of Swiss **Gruyère** or French **Comté**: deep, smooth, and fruity, often redolent of pineapple. Emphasize that breath of toffee with a fruitier red like Valpolicella or a more succulent California Cab.

LIVAROT

FRANCE | RAW/PASTEURIZED | WASHED RIND | A.O.C.

An unfortunate thing about life in the United States is that The Colonel conjures images of greasy fried chicken. In Normandy, *le colonel* is a fat, squashy patty of Livarot, so nicknamed because its binding of five strips of rush (or paper) resembles the stripes on an army colonel's jacket. It's a heavy, moist, semisoft cheese, in its finest incarnation tasting of roasted garlic and cured meat.

Avoid overly ammoniated, cracked, or otherwise offensive wheels. The nutty, savory, buttery paste of this classic is cloaked in a thin, orange rind colored with roucou. Deeper and more nuanced than some of the real stinkies, its pungency can be further tempered by removing the rind. Tradition dictates Calvados, which works, but try a dry, toasty, hard cider for a brilliant (and also regionally inspired) pairing. Widely available Woodchuck will do, but seek out a Norman French producer for real magic.

LIVELY RUN CAYUGA BLUE

USA | RAW | BLUE | VEGETARIAN

In a town called Interlaken, just outside Ithaca, New York, in the Finger Lakes, Lively Run produces this beautiful, subdued, farmstead blue with veins as deep as the lake it's named for. The Messmers—Steve, a native of Interlaken, and Susanne, a native of Germany (who spent childhood summers near cheese-laden Alsace), maintain and milk a herd of about 120 goats: Alpines, Nubians, and a cross of the two breeds. Aged just over sixty days, this cheese has a predominant flavor of sweet, clean, nutty goat milk with a faint residual kick from the blue that just starts to develop. Never goaty, always delicate, it's well suited to the local Riesling portfolio.

LLANGLOFFAN

WALES | RAW | FIRM

After a career playing viola for the Halle orchestra, Welshman Leon Downey was worried he'd become bored with his job and begin to hate music, so he turned to cheesemaking and began producing this hard, dry sister to classic English **Cheshire**. He's riffed on an old familiar recipe, creating a surprisingly full, rich version of the normally lactic, tangy, flaking Cheshire (minus the orange hue). Prepare for a bit of fire on the finish, concentrated at the tip of the tongue, and an overall grassiness that comes from cheese made only in the summer, when the cows are eating verdant, juicy grasses. Look for a lighter red, like Pinot Noir, to fully appreciate the cheese's buttery concentration.

LORD OF THE HUNDREDS

ENGLAND | RAW | FIRM | VEGETARIAN

Centuries before James Aldridge began making this cheese, the first Saxon magistrates collected taxes at Hundreds Knoll in Sussex, and likely made quite a killing. Today, this sweet, crusty-pasted delight won't tax your palate. We first sought it as an alternative to better-known **Berkswell**, but its mild-mannered fattiness and blocky shape make it a contender in its own right. Enduringly sweet, like the rich English grasses that fueled its creation, it is an ideal companion for many reds, from Italian Barolo to Chianti Classico.

LOVETREE TRADE LAKE CEDAR

USA | RAW | SEMISOFT | VEGETARIAN

Mary Falk and her husband, David, produce a selection of pristine raw milk cheeses from their northern Wisconsin herd of sheep. Of particular note is this natural-rind cheese aged on cedar boughs in their aging cave. As Mary describes it, the local *toolie fog* seeps into the cave each morning, bringing the sweet, spicy aromas of wild lilac, evergreen, mustard grass, violet, clover, and sweet milkweed. Expect a fruity, nutty flavor that ends with a distinct woodsiness to the silky, semi-soft paste. We like it with the steelier Chardonnays coming out of Oregon.

MACONNAIS

FRANCE | RAW | FRESH

From Burgundy comes this austere little nugget. Blanketed in a downy coat of blue, gray, and green molds, with an interior paste like spun cream, this raw goat cheese is a tiny treasure. Silky, light flavors of grass and fresh milk make it an ideal companion to the steelier varieties of Burgundian Chardonnay. We gravitate to specimens aged by Hervé Mons; each drum reminds us of goat cheese the way it tastes in France.

MAHON

SPAIN | RAW/PASTEURIZED | HARD | D.O.

You can spot the real deal because the top of this rust-colored square juts up like a moldy Hershey's Kiss. Mahon is wrapped in a square of cloth during pressing, where the folds and creases create little nooks in the rind that capture a heady aroma of fir trees, apricots, and salty ocean water. No wonder: The windswept island of Minorca's pastures are regularly bathed in sea foam. The result is an intense, salty, cakey-pasted miracle, aged in underground caves by the island's skilled *recogedores-afinadores* (gatherers-ripeners). We avoid the "extra aged" versions, which offer some neat butterscotch and spice notes, but none of the punch-in-the-eye intensity we expect. Definitely avoid the version coated in Day-Glo orange plastic. Choose a wine with tons of fruit—from California Chardonnay to Merlot or, preferably, a sweet Madeira or port.

MAJOR FARM VERMONT SHEPHERD

USA | RAW | FIRM

David and Cindy Major are true American pioneers. Not in the covered wagon sense, but in the farmstead cheesemaking sense. After making their first cheeses, which they describe as "horrible," the Majors decided to try a different tactic. They began with a trip to the French Pyrénées, and, inspired by the glorious pressed sheep-milk cheeses, set out to make something similar in Putney, Vermont. A wheel from their inaugural batch was sent to the 1993 American Cheese Society conference, where it won first prize in the Farmhouse Division. Vermont Shepherd has taken numerous awards since. Back home in Vermont, Cindy and David have trained others in the art of making sheep cheese, helping to preserve small-scale Vermont agriculture and enable farmers to achieve a greater profit from their labor by selling artisanal cheese.

Available from late August until reserves are depleted around Easter, Vermont Shepherd has that signature paste: dense but smooth, and round with fat in the mouth. Each batch is different, displaying flavors of wild thyme, hints of mint, and rich nuttiness near the rough, brushed rind. This delicate complexity of flavor finds harmonious pairing with fruitier wines; we especially like Beaujolais or Pinot Noir.

MANCHEGO (QUESO MANCHEGO)
SPAIN | RAW/PASTEURIZED | FIRM | D.O.

This is it: the one that put Spain on the map for cheese-eating Americans who can't get enough of their "Man-chan-go." (Please note, there's no *n* in the middle, so it's *che*, as in Guevara.) The signature rind is thick and waxed, covered with a zigzag pattern impressed by the molds in which the wheels are formed. This cheese from La Mancha offers a full spectrum of flavor: Young, pasteurized wheels can be quite bland, but smaller-production versions are satisfyingly dense, mild, and a bit grassy and fatty. With age the increasingly brittle flesh maintains that creamy character; the taste is more briny nuttiness and increasingly sharp, though never ferocious. True adventurers can seek out the oil-cured wheels, choice specimens that spend their lives bathed in extra virgin olive oil, which prevents the formation of a rind and thus helps maintain a chunkier, fleshy paste and fruity, piquant flavor. Manchego is traditionally paired with sticky *membrillo* (quince paste) and a glass of Crianza Rioja.

MANOURI OR
GREECE | PASTEURIZED | FIRM

Coming all the "whey" from Greece—Thessalia and central and western Macedonia, where it is spelled *Manoypi*—this bright white freshie is similar to **Ricotta Salata** (another cheese made from whey), except Manouri is far less salty and tangy. Rindless and consistently creamy-flaky from end to end, it is like an aged sheep- or goat-milk cream cheese. A hint of lemon-citrus sneaks up on you as the meltingly smooth, sweet paste soothes your palate; the best way to serve it is with figs and apricots, fresh or preserved, but it also enhances tomato-based dishes.

MAROILLES

FRANCE | RAW | WASHED RIND | A.O.C.

This sticky, noxious block, nicknamed *vieux puant* (old stinker), dates back to 962, when it was created by monks in the northern region of Nord-Pas-de-Calais. Looking and smelling like **Pont-l'Evêque**, Maroilles is the bossier older sibling, far outweighing le Pont in pungency. The A.O.C. covers three sizes, and though each can age for an exceptionally long time (120 or so days for the largest, one-pound variety), we prefer the smaller eight-ounce blocks, with their oozing, melting paste and heady, barny aromas. Not for the faint of heart, Maroilles is the commander in chief of the imposing army of stinkdom: aggressive and lingering, with that distinctive earth/petrol flavor. Try intense Calvados for an excuse to drink brandy while it's still light out.

MAXIDOME CHÈVRE

FRANCE | PASTEURIZED | BLOOMY

The name says it all: big goat dome. Earthy and far less tangy than most chèvres, the two-textured paste is runny under the edible, bloomy rind and

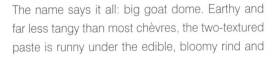

firm at the center. A few months of aging concentrates the flavor of the flaky interior, with its whiff of straw and mushroom, making the Maxidome a particularly suitable choice for those who dislike tangy, lemony fresh goat cheese. It's from Poitou, courtesy of the final foreign invaders, the Saracens, who were shown the door in 732, but whose goats were invited to stay. Get yourself a Vouvray for sweet compatibility.

MAYTAG BLUE

USA | RAW | BLUE

Legend has it that during the Great Depression, when most people weren't buying new appliances, the Maytag family decided to invest in dairy cows as a sort of insurance policy, since people always need milk. Newton, Iowa, home of the appliance factory, is ideal for cows, but to make money, the Maytags had to make cheese. With the help of Iowa State University, a **Roquefort**-inspired blue was produced. Entirely handmade, Maytag Blue has never been advertised, building its reputation through word of mouth. Upon tasting, you will see why. Its rich, creamy texture is assertive and piquant, with a long linger. Works for a world-class blue cheese dip or dressing, too. As a sweet counterpoint, pair it with a tawny or vintage port.

MEADOW CREEK GRAYSON

USA | RAW | WASHED RIND

Galax, Virginia's Feete family uses ecologically sound farming practices in raising their herd of Jersey cows: No pesticides or herbicides are used in the fields where the cows are rotationally pastured; the cows are never confined or fed silage, and are given minimal hormones and antibiotics; and the milking season ends when grass growth wanes and the cows wind down their milk production. The quality of the cheese reflects this diligence. The brownish-orange rind of each mildly pungent four-pound block covers a supple, semisoft paste that is rich and beefy with distinctive, sweet nuttiness. The cheeses made from lighter, less fatty spring and summer milk do well with a fresh pale ale. Late-autumn milk produces a huskier cheese that we prefer with a stout brown beer.

MILLEENS

IRELAND | PASTEURIZED | WASHED RIND

She set out to protest "supermarket cheese" and came up with something special. Veronica Steele, at the urging of her husband, Norman, and with the milk of a one-horned cow named Brisket, initiated modern-day Irish farmstead cheesemaking in county Cork. Later, more cows were obtained, and Norman quit his day job to help run the farm. These days, son Quinlan has taken over production, so Veronica can busy herself teaching more Irishwomen to make cheese, as she has done with Giana Ferguson, maker of **Gubbeen**, and Jeffa Gill, maker of **Durrus**. Milleens is a cheese that varies depending on season and wheel size, but always with one constant: the Platonic ideal of a good washed rind. The rind varies in color from mottled peach to fiery orange; the paste may be semifirm to spilling cream; the flavor begins mellow, but with age becomes assertive. In each stage of maturation, Milleen embodies the range of what pungent, meaty, occasionally aggressive cheese can be. A soft Chenin Blanc will soothe your palate.

MIMOLETTE 🐄

FRANCE | PASTEURIZED | HARD

Mimolette has an ugly little secret: As it matures, it houses microscopic little nits called cheese mites. Though small, they are choosy, preferring dark, damp places with minimal airflow, where they can gorge themselves silly on the rinds of developing cheese. The beauty is that their tunneling and nibbling promote airflow and flavor development in many aged cheeses. In this case, start with a big bowling-ball-shaped wheel. Then give the wheel eighteen to twenty-four months to mature into a mite-ridden cannonball with craters deep enough to stick your fingertip in. Have no fear, the mites have departed by the time you eat the cheese, and you'd be loath to eat the rock-hard crust of a rind, anyway. Beneath its shell, Mimolette has waxen paste of neon-orange hue that sticks to the teeth with an intense caramelized sweetness. There's a dispute over whether this oddball was created by the French or the Dutch. It's likely French cheesemakers "created" Mimolette using a Dutch recipe. Try the Malbec-based wines of southern France and Argentina.

MONTASIO 🐄

ITALY | RAW | FIRM | D.O.P.

Made exclusively from the milk of dairy farms in Friuli-Venezia-Giulia, the northeastern corner of

Italy, this firm, straw-yellow wheel matures into a dry, flaking paste with a mild, slightly nutty character. Montasio is most popularly used in *frico,* a crisp snack prepared by grating the cheese and cooking it in a searing hot pan—an impressive hors d'oeuvre or accompaniment to a green salad. On its own, Montasio is comparable to neighboring **Asiago d'Allevo**: a straightforward table cheese that we like with rustic red wine, such as Sangiovese, though the more obscure Friulian whites are delicate, refreshing partners.

MONTE ENEBRO (QUESO DEL TIETAR)

SPAIN | PASTEURIZED | SEMISOFT

Made by a single producer, Rafael Báez of Ávila in Castilla y León, this bizarre and exuberant goat cheese is shaped like a log, but is said to resemble the leg of a mule. A rind composed of ash and mold means insistent flavor, more like a blue cheese than anything else. The damp, cakey, acidic paste near the rind is fierce, with unmistakable overtones of black walnut. Inside, the core remains salty, lactic, and soothing. A relatively new cheese on the scene, Monte Enebro was awarded the distinction of top goat cheese in Spain in 2003. That insistent flavor is pacified by sweeter wines made from the charming Muscat grape.

MORBIER

FRANCE | RAW/PASTEURIZED | SEMISOFT

Morbier is from the eponymous town in the Jura Mountains, where wheels were traditionally made from two milkings, evening and morning, separated by a layer of ash. The story goes that **Comté** cheesemakers with extra curds at the end of each day stored them in large pans and sprinkled them with soot to protect their bounty from flies until they could add curds the following morning to make small wheels for personal consumption. Thus by accident was born the semisoft, pressed, and uncooked cheese with the pronounced aroma and hearty flavor that is Morbier. Today the layer is one of vegetable ash, usually decorative, and the paste remains supple and sweet. There are industrial and artisanal producers. The hallmark of truly fine farmhouse production is a thick, creamy texture and sweet, milky finish. Look for gently bulging sides, a lightly sticky orange rind, and an irregular smattering of small holes. Here you have a classic partner for a lush red Rhône.

MORNING FRESH DAIRY BLUE

USA | PASTEURIZED | BLUE

Morning Fresh Dairy has been in the Graves family of Bellvue, Colorado, for nearly four generations, delivering milk in glass bottles since 1894. The story of this nascent blue begins with the disappointing closure of Bingham Hill farm in Fort Collins. An assistant cheesemaker took the recipe for Bingham Hill Blue and went looking for good milk: This mixed herd of four hundred Holsteins and Jerseys graze on thousands of open acres. A modification of that Bingham Hill recipe makes a squat little square of dense, fudgy blue. Its unsweetened chocolate taste pairs well with the deep, cooked-fruitiness of Madeira.

MOZZARELLA

ITALY | PASTEURIZED | FRESH

There's more to mozzarella than that tasteless white stuff atop your fast-food pizza, or those plasticky blocks provided by Polly-O. Real, fresh mozzarella can bring you to your knees; it is *pasta filata*, or "pulled-curd," cheese. By pulling mozzarella curd, shredding it on a *chitarra* (guitar), plunking this into nearly boiling water, and then continually stretching and pulling it with a paddle, cheesemakers produce a smooth, stretchy, rindless ball. Once a mass has formed, it's *mozzare* (torn) and re-formed into various shapes.

This pulled-curd cheese, historically produced in the southern Italian regions of Campania, Lazio, and Apulia, now takes fine shape in the United States. In New York, our one-pound balls of fresh and smoked mozzarella arrive from Joe's Dairy on nearby Sullivan Street. When we're lucky enough to arrive early, our reward is mozzarella so fresh it's still warm, and swimming in a thin sea of butterfat under its plastic wrapping. It's heaven in the cold weather on toasted bread, and perfectly paired in the warm summer with fat tomatoes and basil.

The curds can be molded into various shapes and sizes. Our two favorites are *bocconcini* and *ciliegini*. Picture little cotton balls, but solid and made of lightly salted, yielding, and chewy fresh milk. We like them seasoned—tossed with extra virgin olive oil, slivers of garlic, red pepper flakes, and a handful of chopped fresh parsley.

BURRATA

ITALY | PASTEURIZED | FRESH

Here's a way to blow your friends' minds with a spoon. As in **mozzarella**, cheese curds are plunged into hot whey until they become elastic, cut into strips, plunged into whey again, kneaded, stretched, and pulled into a smooth ball that weeps butterfat. This ball is left hollow, to be filled with uncooked curds and flakes of mozzarella that spill out when you stab the rindless exterior. That soupy center of uncooked curds continues to ferment, creating a flavor that is gamier and stronger than mozzarella's. Grab a spoon, some Italian bread, and a bottle of rich, contemporary-style Soave, and have a party.

MOZZARELLA DI BUFALA CAMPANA

WATER BUFFALO | ITALY | PASTEURIZED | FRESH | D.O.P.

Here's the real deal, which has been around since before cows came on the scene. The bulk of production comes from Campania, Lazio, and Apulia, though production dates back to seventh-century Campania. It is made like cow's-milk mozzarella, but of stronger-tasting milk that's three times fattier and imparts a slightly sour, gamy flavor. Unlike cow's-milk mozzarella, which stiffens with age, mozzarella di bufala continues to break down until it becomes mushy, which means it's too old. Serve drizzled with fine, grassy olive oil, tomato, and basil or make phenomenal eggplant parmigiano, pizza, or lasagna. It's the classic choice for true Neapolitan pizza. Enjoy with whatever white or red you've bought for your dinner.

The Magazine for Responsible Horse Owners ®

HORSE
ILLUSTRATED

P.O. Box 57549, Boulder, CO 80322-7549

MOZZARELLA COMPANY HOJA SANTA 🐐

USA | PASTEURIZED | FRESH | VEGETARIAN

Made with goat's milk collected from local farmers around Dallas, Texas, Hoja Santa is allowed to set overnight. The following day it is hand molded and drained, salted, and then turned for several days. The little pucks of tangy, fresh cheese are then wrapped in a local herb, *hoja santa*, which means "holy leaf." Traditionally, the herb is used to wrap fish and chicken in Mexican cuisine. The edible leaf imparts a minty, sarsaparilla flavor that brightens the existing citrus qualities in the cheese. We find it ideal for warmer weather, when clean, zesty flavors are preferred such as Sauvignon Blanc.

MUNSTER/MUNSTER-GÉROMÉ 🐄

FRANCE | RAW/PASTEURIZED | WASHED RIND | A.O.C.

Don't be confused: This is not the deli-counter cheese with sprayed-on orange dye but the famous (and famously stinky) Munster from northeastern France. Made on both sides of the Vosges Mountains (Alsace in the east, Lorraine in the west), this aromatic softie is washed in brine until it has the consistency of melting chocolate. You can thank the high-protein milk of the Vosgiennes cows for that. The sticky interior, with its sweet milkiness, rewards those willing to brave the smell. Though we can get the pasteurized versions here, their gummy, acrid, unpleasant tang bears little resemblance to the great raw milk versions. It's classically served with toasted cumin seeds and a local, floral Gewürztraminer.

NETTLE MEADOW KUNIK

USA | PASTEURIZED | BLOOMY

In New York's southern Adirondacks, Sheila Flanagan makes this tart, tangy triple crème with pasteurized goat's milk, but enriches it with fatty Jersey cow's cream. The blend makes for a sumptuous, buttery paste that retains the kick of fresh chevre. A bit lemony but plenty of that mushroom and wet straw we look for in good bloomy rinds. To mix up our usual equation of triple crème/sparkling wine, look for the sweet peachiness of sparkling Chenin Blanc.

NEVAT

SPAIN | PASTEURIZED | BLOOMY

Spain's northwest corner is famous for **Tetilla**, so named for its breastlike shape. Produced to the east in Catalonia is the nipple, Nevat, which literally translates as "snowy." The G-rated description would be an enormous white Hershey's Kiss, but either way you get the picture. Thanks to the molds on the mild, edible white rind, the cheese matures from the outside in, becoming tangy and oozing around the flaky white core. When Nevat is young, the flavor is delicate, clean, a bit powdery. Pairing with Albariño heightens the passion.

OAKVALE FARMHOUSE GOUDA

USA | RAW | SEMISOFT

From this small family farm in Madison County, Ohio, comes an ideal Gouda. Made from the milk of eighty cows (mainly Holsteins, with a few Brown Swiss and Jerseys) that roam freely through pastures, here is the retort to pasteurized, processed supermarket Gouda. Firm and smooth, with a satisfying, fatty paste, Oakvale captures the sweet, nutty tang that is younger Gouda's hallmark. You could certainly melt it down for superlative omelets, but it's good enough to eat by the wedge with rough wheat crackers and a round, buttery California Chardonnay.

OKA

CANADA | RAW/PASTEURIZED | WASHED RIND

Canada's version of a washed-rind cheese isn't strong and complex. Oka is washed in brine, and the rind is really pungent, but the buttery, semisoft paste is mild and satisfyingly nutty. Somewhere along the way it got the reputation of being made from partially skimmed milk and of being low fat. It's not. So since you're not watching your weight, have a beer of the sort that inspired washed-rind cheeses in the first place: a dark, frothy Chimay or another monastery-produced Trappist brew.

OLD CHATHAM CAMEMBERT

USA | PASTEURIZED | BLOOMY | VEGETARIAN

Few American cheese producers are as familiar as Old Chatham Sheepherding Company. The little black ewe on a verdant green label burst onto the gourmet market and restaurant scene in New York in 1994 and has been gaining ground ever since. But is this Camembert? It's square,

American, and made of sheep's and cow's milk. This ain't like any French Camembert we know. It just isn't as runny and mushroomy as the good French versions. It is, however, intensely creamy, sweet, and mild. A gentler Camembert, best enjoyed with softer wines like white Bordeaux.

OLD CHATHAM SHEPHERD'S WHEEL

USA | PASTEURIZED | BLOOMY | VEGETARIAN

Old Chatham began with 115 East Friesian sheep, and the flock has grown to well over a thousand. To dictate lambing (and thus control milking), the folks at Old Chatham need to overcome sheep's natural inclination to mate in the fall. They do this by exposing the flock to artificial light twenty-two hours a day during the fall and winter months; when the sheep go out to pasture in March, a group of ten rams is brought in to impregnate designated sheep in the flock. The so-called ram effect, on the heels of extended light, appears to be quite successful, resulting in pregnant sheep, bountiful milk, and the classic sheepy Shepherd's Wheel. This buttercreamy, sweet, mild wheel has none of the gamy, lanolin notes that can be the downfall of sheep cheese. Travel just as far as New York's Finger Lakes for a lovely little Riesling.

OSSAU-IRATY-BREBIS PYRÉNÉES

FRANCE | RAW | FIRM | A.O.C.

We've always been partial to blondes, even those of a certain age, and this is the oldest blonde we know. Most records indicate that the Ossau-Iraty cheeses from Aquitaine were among the first cheeses ever made—thousands of years ago. Legend has it that Aristee, the shepherder son of Apollo, created the Ossau-Iraty cheese. After all this time, she still looks good. The thick, buff rind is dappled with rust and gray molds; beneath, the ivory paste is slightly grainy, but Botoxed with butterfat. Despite its elegant, wheat-flour aroma, the fat is unapologetic. This dense richness is most pronounced in the floral milk of late summer. Meaning: Wheels that are available six to eight months later (March–May) are supreme. There are many versions to keep an eye out for, the most prevalent being Abbaye de Belloc, produced by the Benedictine monks of the Belloc Abbey in the western Pyrénées. Other popular imitators, produced on a larger scale and made of pasteurized milk (not qualifying for the A.O.C.), are the simple, pleasing, and good "starter" cheeses Doux de Montagne, Etorki, and Prince de Claverolle. The cheese's grassy sweetness is heightened by a smoky Pouilly-Fumé.

PYRÉNÉES BREBIS

FRANCE | RAW | FIRM

From the Basque region, where separatists fight for autonomy from both France and Spain, comes one of the most agreeable cheeses we sell, one that is wholeheartedly recommended by many a Murray's cheesemonger. With a balanced and complex range of flavors, Brebis is sweet to the point of caramelization, at once grassy and hazelnutty. It's one of those rare cheeses enjoyed by neophytes and "cheese snobs" alike. Aged for four to six months, the natural rind surrounds a firm, dense, ivory paste that is smooth with butter-fat. Although this cheese is available year-round, we highly recommend it during the spring, when it is made from the highly floral autumn milk. It bears many similarities to the name-protected **Ossau-Iraty**, but does not fall under the A.O.C. Its texture is more pliable, the flavor rich and honeyed. A full-bodied red with spice, as in Syrah (Shiraz), bal-ances that unctuous sweetness.

OSSERA SERRAT GROS (QUESO DE OSSERA)

SPAIN | RAW | SEMISOFT

There are many advantages to scouring the earth to find good cheese, but this cheese is one of the greatest. In the tiny Pyrénées hamlet of Ossera, Eulália Torras herds a troupe of forty-five goats to a different pasture each day. The reason, she ex-plains, is that they're too picky to eat in the same place twice. Back home, the lone ram, Boc Dylan, waits under a tree for the next lucky lady. The va-riety in the goats' diet is evident in a shifting flavor spectrum that is saline, earthy, musty, lactic, and woodsy, but this highly seasonal treasure always boasts deep, rich flavor and a pronounced goaty tang. Each puck is wrapped in cloth to protect the dense, sticky-clay paste. Sheer, bubbly Catalan Cava cleanses the palate before the next bite.

PAGLIETTA

ITALY | PASTEURIZED | BLOOMY

Hay: It's not just for horses. In Piedmont, *paglia* (hay) is fed to cows whose milk is made into small, voluptuous rounds of cheese. But wait, there's more: According to tradition, these diminutive discs are nestled in a bed of straw during ripening, thus providing beneficial weight, damp heat, and hay aroma for extra flavor. The result is a soft-ripened little treat with earthy, garlicky, nutty tones. Paglietta is only one variety of Paglia cheese, though these oozing patties all share a butter-yellow hue and consistently milky, tangy flavor. Drink some Prosecco for a perfect match.

PARMIGIANO-REGGIANO

ITALY | RAW | HARD | D.O.P.

If you could be a fly on the wall during cheesemongers' therapy sessions, you might hear a recurring nightmare: "I sat down to dinner and asked for Parmigiano. The waiter brought a green cardboard cylinder filled with . . . with . . . I can't go on, it's too painful." And once you've tried the *real* Parmigiano-Reggiano, you'll never go back to that acrid, powdery "Parmesan" either. Every eighty-pound wheel is stamped with the date of production and a repeating "Parmigiano-Reggiano" to verify authenticity. It is worth noting that the leftover whey is fed to the hogs fortunate enough to become future legs of Prosciutto di Parma.

Parmigiano-Reggiano is available at twelve months, but we like it best between twenty and thirty months, depending on the month of production. By then, the café au lait–colored insides have dried to crunchy perfection: nutty, spicy, salty (but not too much so), and floral, with a distinct caramel finish.

Even better than the original is Parmigiano-Reggiano delle Vacche Rosse, made from the exceptionally rich and creamy milk of the rare and once-endangered red cow, and aged anywhere from twelve to twenty-four months. Older isn't always better. We find the rare "super-aged" wheels at three to five years are often sandy, dry, and excessively salty, without the nuanced complexity that makes this cheese great. A sublime cheese, truly at home with the dry berry sparkle of regional Lambrusco.

PATA DE MULO (QUESO PATA DE MULO)

SPAIN | RAW | FIRM

We're not pulling your leg when we tell you this "leg of the mule" is gentle, sweet, and fruity, containing no mule by-products. With an elongated, flattened, cylindrical shape, it recalls its better-known goat cousin, also from Castilla y León: **Monte Enebro (Queso del Tietar)**. Aged for three to four months, the paste is firm yet beautifully supple, with a high butterfat content; the rind is a smooth, pale ochre. It's mild, but substantive, so pair it with something juicy, such as a California Merlot.

PAVÉ D'AUGE

FRANCE | RAW | WASHED RIND

Pavé d'Auge always seems to be blushing, perhaps from being chased in the cool autumn months, after its production from rich summer milk, its salty brine bath, and a few months in a dark, damp cave. We lust after its pungent, buttery paste and deep, bacony flavor. Like a bigger slab of **Pont-l'Evêque**, this farmhouse block is also produced in the northern region of Calvados. Though the flavor is meaty and full, it's never offensive. It's an ideal intro to the world of washed-rinds: light on the salt and stink. The paste is weighty on the tongue—substantial and spicy. Whenever we can catch up with one, we enjoy it with a glass of racy Gewürztraminer.

PEAKED MOUNTAIN EWE JERSEY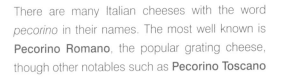

USA | RAW | FIRM

You (no pun intended) will love Bob and Ann Workses' mixed-milk variant of the famed **Vermont Shepherd**. Bob and Ann moved to Townsend, Vermont, from Manhattan and were some of the first aspiring cheesemakers to blossom under the tutelage of Cindy and David Major. This pressed cheese is aged for four to six months, its buff rind protecting the dense, smooth, butterfatty paste—simple but incredibly delicious. A richer, more mellow variation on French Pyrénées mountain tommes like **Ossau-Iraty**, this farmstead round offers hearty, herby flavors, with grassy undertones in the satisfyingly meaty texture. It's brilliant with a wide range of reds and whites, but especially those with some fruit, from Chardonnay to Beaujolais.

PECORINO

ITALY

There are many Italian cheeses with the word *pecorino* in their names. The most well known is **Pecorino Romano**, the popular grating cheese, though other notables such as **Pecorino Toscano** are climbing to the top of the cheese counter. Taken from the Italian *pecora*, meaning "sheep," and *ino*, meaning "little," you've got a little sheep cheese.

Most villages in Italy have at least one cheese to call their own, and for many, that cheese is a pecorino, some dating as far back as 25 B.C. Some say pecorinos were the first cheeses: A shepherd, preparing for a journey, put some sheep's milk in a bag made from a sheep's stomach. As the milk shook within the enzyme-laden pouch, it began to solidify. With a few hours' time, heat, and movement, that milk became something much greater, as we are about to see . . .

PECORINO CROTONESE

ITALY | PASTEURIZED | FIRM

A-tisket, a-tasket, aged in a wicker basket. Look for proof of identity in the ridged, textured rind and the woody, vegetal flavors that balance its salty sharpness. With roots in the southern Italian city of Crotone, it is now made in Sardinia and Rome. As befits a peacock of a cheese, the rind has a smattering of purple and orange technicolor molds. Made from January to June when the milk is best and most abundant, and aged for a minimum of three months, this is firm enough for grating and tasty enough to enjoy as a table cheese with a red such as Cabernet Sauvignon.

PECORINO DI FOSSA

ITALY | RAW | SEMISOFT

When the Sogliano sul Rubicone region of Emilia-Romagna was raided in the twelfth century, it was hide the cheese or starve. Rounds of sheep's or cow's milk were squirreled away in cloth sacks and buried in wells dug in the soft tufa soil. In nearly 100 percent humidity and temperatures up to 70 degrees, the cheese fermented, developing a lumpy, deformed appearance, no rind to speak of, and a strong, musky flavor complemented by aromas of wet leaves.

The Saracens have since departed, but the cheese is still produced annually, buried in August and unearthed three months later, on November 25, in celebration of St. Catherine's Day. While the moniker *formaggio di fossa* is a catchall for cheese buried in this manner, look for authentic Pecorino di Fossa, from the wells in Sogliano sul Rubicone. A formidable red such as Sangiovese or the fruity sparkle of local Lambrusco is necessary to temper the slightly bitter, crumbly paste.

PECORINO DI PIENZA
ITALY | RAW/PASTEURIZED | FIRM

From Pienza, Tuscany, comes this exquisitely beautiful artisanal cheese, aged one to two months. Firm yet pliable in the mouth, it has an admirable balance between the delicate tang of a young sheep's-milk cheese and the sweet, earthy, hazelnut flavors of a more aged wheel. Its wheat-colored, buttery flesh contrasts with the soft, tomatoey, fully edible exterior, offering the one-two flavor punch of sweet/milky against tart/acidic. Complete the picture with a bottle of rich, round Soave.

PECORINO FOGLIE DE NOCE
ITALY | RAW/PASTEURIZED | FIRM

Pleasing to both the eye and the palate, Foglie de Noce has the occasional walnut leaf adhering to its nubbly black rind. Roughly the size and shape of an ostrich egg, each infant cheese is bathed and turned daily for three weeks. As adolescents they are put in barrels for several months and separated with layers of walnut leaves, which impart an astringent, vegetal flavor. The mature cheese has a walnutty, lightly peppery taste and a firm, sometimes flaky texture. The high butterfat content serves to carry the flavor. That spicy finish likes a softer red like Italian Valpolicella.

PECORINO GINEPRO

ITALY | RAW | FIRM

In the region of Lazio, these six-pound wheels are submerged in an aromatic bath of balsamic vinegar and juniper berries to age for a minimum of four months. The vinegar creates a crunchy, bittersweet-chocolate-looking rind, and the juniper gives the astringent nip of gin. Like all good sheep's-milk cheeses, an underlying sweetness lingers within the mellow, lanolin finish. Wrapped in moist paper, the crust arrives with a dusting of powdery green mold; this cheese benefits from a few hours' breathing before it's cut. You could let that bottle of Nebbiolo breathe, too, while you wait.

PECORINO IMPERATORE

ITALY | PASTEURIZED | FIRM

Sardinia, the second-largest island in the Mediterranean, is known for its hearty aged sheep's-milk cheeses. Standing tall in its basket-molded sturdiness, Pecorino Imperatore threatens to assault the palate. But the dusky rind and firm, crumbly paste belie its delicate nature. The flavor here is soft and sweet, with a musky aroma. Dense and buttery against a rough, rustic red, Imperatore provides an opportunity to experiment with a dark, plummy Sardinian wine like Carmignano.

PECORINO MARZOLINO

ITALY | RAW | SEMISOFT

The exterior is rubbed with the famed San Marzano tomatoes, which, in addition to giving it beautiful color, lend a juicy, vegetal flavor and light, tangy finish. A small, terra-cotta-colored mound with a smooth, supple paste and round, butterfatty texture, it's a distinctive and delightful Tuscan cheese. A glass of crisp, white Orvieto makes it that much better.

PECORINO NERO DI SIENA

ITALY | RAW | SEMISOFT

Translated as the "black sheep of Siena," the moniker refers to the black, spray-wax coating—not unlike that of genuine **Pecorino Romano**—that encases this sweet, nutty Tuscan wheel. The contrast of black rind and bright white paste makes a striking appearance on a cheese board. And it's nothing like the salty, sharp grating cheese most of us associate with pecorino. Incredibly rich and truly succulent with fat, the moist, condensed milk intensity is most expressive with the acidic red wines from the region, including Sangiovese and especially Chianti Classico.

PECORINO ORO ANTICO

ITALY | PASTEURIZED | FIRM

Behold the "Old Gold" (*Oro* = gold, *Antico* = old), made in Tuscany and aged for at least eight months in a cellar, where it is regularly brushed with olive oil. Beneath a rind reminiscent of the "burnt umber" crayon in your childhood box of Crayolas is the golden-hued firm and flaky paste. The flavor offers the agreeable sheep's-milk trifecta: nutty, grassy, and gamy. When you see the red wax seal, you'll know it's the one. You can go Chianti, or go multinational with a glass of Spanish Rioja.

PECORINO PEPATO

ITALY | RAW/PASTEURIZED | FIRM

Chunky, coarse peppercorns give Pepato its zest. Traditionally from Sicily, this cheese comes with a long and fabled history: Romulus was rumored to have made his wheels with goat milk, and in its traditional sheep-milk form it was mentioned in texts as early as the first century A.D. *Pepato* means "with pepper," and whole black peppercorns are distributed throughout the bright white paste for pronounced spiciness. Rindless, the exterior has indentations from pressing in basket molds. Younger wheels remain supple but firm; a golden pallor and dry, crumbly paste mean an older (and saltier) wheel. Best when eaten young, it makes a good shredding cheese; as a table cheese it marries well with dry-cured meats and sausages, and pairs nicely with a spicy red such as Montepulciano.

PECORINO ROMANO

ITALY | PASTEURIZED | FIRM

This cheese was so important it was part of the daily rations for Roman legionaries in the first century A.D. Fulvi, the brand of Pecorino Romano at Murray's, is still traditionally made in Nepi, a village in the Roman countryside; therefore, it is referred to as "genuine" Pecorino Romano. Less hard and dry than its Sardinian-made counterparts, this hearty, full-flavored cheese is handmade according to an ancient recipe and aged naturally in cellars in sixty-five-pound wheels. The finest milk from sheep in the Lazio region, rich in fat and protein, is selected from small producers, analyzed regularly, and kept free of additives or hormones. The cheese has a bold, briny, pungent flavor that beautifully offsets all manner of sweet, acidic tomato sauces. It also is the basis for one of Rome's greatest dishes, *pasta alla gricia*, which is nothing more than spaghetti, Pecorino Romano, and pepper, but totally perfect. A bright California Merlot would play off the salty tang.

PECORINO TARTUFELLO

ITALY | RAW | SEMISOFT

Those enterprising Toscani tarted up one of their many sheep cheeses with generous slabs of black truffle. Younger wheels are smooth, buttery, and rindless; more aged versions are flaky beneath a hard crust. Both have the damp, earthen aroma of fungi. The creaminess of younger varieties is straight-up sexy, while the heady flavor of truffle in older wheels is leaner and more restrained. Both are intensely satisfying, especially when coupled with a Tuscan red such as Sangiovese.

PECORINO TOSCANO

ITALY | RAW/PASTEURIZED | SEMISOFT OR FIRM

This pale, bright, rindless wheel bears so little resemblance to its aged counterpart that it's difficult to believe they are essentially the same cheese. Aged for only thirty to sixty days, its semisoft paste has the bounce of a firm mattress. This clean and mildly tangy treat partners beautifully with fatty, salty, dried *salumeria*. If you like white wine, choose Vernaccia; if red suits your fancy, go with the foreign grape–based wines of Cortona.

Stagionato, or aged Toscano, is rough and rugged with maturity. Aged for six to twelve months, with a sheepy, nutty, olivey edge and a slight degree of sharpness that can come only with age, it has less of a briny sting than pecorinos from other locales. Look for the natural rind: fairly smooth, caramel-colored, with chocolate-brown brushstrokes and a stamp pressed into the side to verify its authenticity. This rustic round makes a fine dessert cheese to serve with honey, figs, and the big, round flavors of locally grown Sangiovese grapes, in liquid form.

PÉLARDON

FRANCE | RAW | BLOOMY

Pélardon is local slang for "pieces," and more generally in the Cévannes region means "small goat cheese." Fitting the definition on both counts, this little piece of chèvre weighs in at just two ounces. Aged for two to three weeks in the southern region of Languedoc-Roussillon, this little chèvre has a mold-ripened rind that encloses a compact paste tasting rich, nutty, and milky, with a lingering, goaty finish. We suggest a big glass of Riesling to pair with this diminutive round.

PÉRAIL
FRANCE | RAW | BLOOMY

After four weeks of aging, Pérail just runs all over your plate, so you'll want to scoop up its lush, savory paste and tangy, sheepy flavor with some crusty bread. Made in the Causses du Larzac, near the town of Roquefort, Pérail uses the same sheep's milk supplied to Roquefort producers from December through June. The chalky soil and rugged terrain are the ideal habitat for sheep. This tiny medallion has a similar appearance to **Saint-Félicien** and **Saint-Marcellin**: small and flat, with a crinkled, bloomy rind. Available after only ten to fifteen days, the pucks are firm and smooth when young; after three weeks their interior becomes milky and melting; and at four weeks, they're off and running. Chase one with a glass of Beaujolais, or if white's your thing, a brisk Chardonnay from Burgundy pairs nicely.

PERAL (QUESO DE PERAL)
SPAIN | PASTEURIZED | BLUE

Rare and unusual, this comparatively new Spanish cheese was created in Asturias near the end of the nineteenth century by a dairy farmer who added a shot of sheep's-milk cream to his cow's milk for extra richness. The cylinders of cheese are ripened in caves where *Penicillium* molds flourish, although sometimes Peral is found with little to no blueing; even then, the damp, fudgy paste is intense. Reminiscent of a washed-rind, Peral features barnyardy aromas and a funky taste, with a bit of buttermilk, salt, and spice in the blue mold. A spicy Syrah cuts the cream and heightens the peppery character.

PERSILLÉ DE CHÈVRE DU BEAUJOLAIS
FRANCE | RAW | BLUE

In French, *persillé* means "parsley," referring to the blue-green fingers of mold that vein blue cheese. This particular Persillé is made by a solitary producer in the Rhône-Alpes, then aged for two to five months in a humid cave. Denser than many blues, the goat's-milk paste provides exceptional texture and flavor: dense and sweet, almost chocolaty. Pockmarks of mold contain a burning spiciness. Add a bottle of German Eiswein (ice wine) and enter the land of Euphoria.

PERSILLÉ DE MALZIEU
FRANCE | RAW | BLUE

Spice is the variety of life, which is why we hunger for this rare, powerfully spicy blue. Produced just beyond the legally protected limits of Roquefort, these wheels are made of Lacaune sheep milk, like their more famous neighbor, but capture a far greater flavor spectrum. Texturally, it sits heavy on the tongue, only to dissolve into a milky skim within seconds. The threat of excess salt, razing sharpness, and intense moldiness is present but always at bay. Beautifully balanced with rich, fatty milk, mushroom, and a long sweetness that is complemented by a rich, oily dessert wine such as Sauternes or tawny port.

PERSILLÉ DU BEAUJOLAIS

FRANCE | RAW | BLUE

Who needs a martini when you can have spiciness and a juniper finish in a cheese? This firm, buttery cylinder looks like the mild, curdy delight **Fourme d'Ambert**, but do not be deceived. Beneath that smooth, dusty rind is a firmer paste with straw-yellow color. Again, *persillé* means it's "parsleyed" with the battleship-gray mold of *Penicillium roqueforti*. Made in the Rhône-Alpes and cave aged, it's best consumed with a glass of nobly rotted Sauternes, or, like the name says, a locally produced Beaujolais.

PETIT BILLY

FRANCE | PASTEURIZED | FRESH

You can slip this "little billy goat" to your friends who claim not to like goat cheese. Feed them Petit Billy from the Loire Valley, and watch their pleasantly surprised reactions. These fresh little cakes of rindless, creamy, youthful goodness are incredibly light, with a pleasant lactic tang. Best enjoyed in the summer because goats typically mate in the fall, and winter cheeses may be made with flavorless frozen curd. Clean and mild, and easily identifiable by the long green leaf (sometimes made of paper) encircling the cheese. Choose a regional grassy white wine like Sauvignon Blanc for crisp, refreshing companionship.

PIAVE

ITALY | PASTEURIZED | HARD

Here's a cheese with a heart of gold—hard and rough on the surface and sweetly nutty underneath. With its dry, crunchy texture, its flavors of tropical fruit and almonds, and its long, sweet finish, this popular favorite is likened to the king of Italian cheese—**Parmigiano-Reggiano**. Ages range from six to fourteen months; seek out the older "Vecchio" production. Piave is wonderful as a table cheese, shaved over a salad of bitter greens, or enjoyed with an aperitif. Like Parmigiano, Piave has an affinity for both red and white wine, but we especially enjoy a fruity Merlot to emphasize the nutty, concentrated kick.

PIERRE-ROBERT

FRANCE | PASTEURIZED | BLOOMY

Cheesemaker Robert Rouzaire forever sealed his amity with his friend Pierre when he created a cheese named for them both: Pierre-Robert. Fittingly, this is a friendly cheese: soft-ripened, with a white, bloomy exterior and a crowd-pleasing, mousselike paste. It's even enriched with cream for true triple-crème decadence. Mild and buttery, there is enough salt and tang to give it a rich flavor. Made in the **Brie** capital of the world, Ile-de-France, this is lovely with yeasty Champagne.

PODDA CLASSICO

ITALY | PASTEURIZED | HARD

One bite and you'll be zapped by the intensity of this mixed-milk offering from the island of Sardinia. Aged for nearly a year, giving it a crumbly, slightly crunchy texture, it's sweet and nutty, with the toffee inclinations of good **Parmigiano-Reggiano**. Without Parm's quarter-inch waxen crust of protective rind, the texture is not great for shaving, so just eat a hunk. Pairing it with anything other than a big red such as Barolo, Barbaresco, or California Cabernet would be folly, as it will run roughshod over anything lighter.

POINT REYES FARMSTEAD CHEESE COMPANY ORIGINAL BLUE, MONTY'S RESERVE

USA | RAW | BLUE | VEGETARIAN

Monty McIntire is now at Point Reyes Station, California, but for ten years he was the cheesemaker for **Maytag Blue**. The man knows blue cheese and was instrumental in the creation of this, California's first commercially available blue cheese. Made from the milk of Holstein cows, the punchy, slightly metallic reserve is aged for a full year, while the standard Original Blue is aged for five to six months. Some liken it to **Roquefort**, with an initial intensity that dissipates into salty milkiness. We find it's more aggressive—biting and tart—with a flavor deeply affected by its proximity to salty Pacific air. This cheese, with its minimal veining and dry, fudgy texture, crumbles nicely into your salad or can be drizzled with honey for a fine dessert. To drink, try a California late-harvest Riesling.

PONT-L'EVÊQUE 🐄

FRANCE | RAW/PASTEURIZED | WASHED RIND | A.O.C.

A hearty little classic that conveniently arrives in its own gift box. Moderately pungent but beefy, it's made in Normandy from the same recipe that has been in use since the Middle Ages, when it was invented by monks. Pont-l'Evêque is also identifiable by its orange-yellow rind crosshatched from a four- to six-week maturation on a woven grille in humid cellars. After several brine washings, the rind becomes insistently aromatic. The paste is plump and resilient, with a mellow, faintly sweet flavor, like buttered popcorn. Remarkable for dessert served with Calvados, the region's famed apple brandy, or a glass of cider (hard or not). The pasteurized version is most prevalent in the United States, and while it is commendable, when you are in France make sure to try it raw.

POULIGNY-SAINT-PIERRE 🐐

FRANCE | RAW | SEMISOFT | A.O.C.

Nicknamed "Tour d'Eiffel" for its shape, this cheese gets its formal name from its town of production, where the uncooked, unpressed goat cheese is ripened on straw mats for fifteen days to five weeks. The cool cellar environment produces a refreshingly herbal cheese that is gentle and milky in youth. With longer aging the paste dries into packed clay. Those initially herbaceous aromas of goat milk and straw intensify into spicy, flinty persistence. Don't fear the mottled, blue rind protecting that snow-white, crumbly, moist paste: Both are delicious to eat. A Loire white made with Sauvignon Blanc grapes accents the fruitiness.

PRIMA DONNA
See **Gouda**

PROVOLONE, AURICCHIO
ITALY | PASTEURIZED | FIRM

Beefy, nutty, and sharp, just like some of Murray's cheesemongers. Born as a company near Naples in 1877, Auricchio quickly became synonymous with sharp **provolone**, thanks to the addition of the company's patented "sharp rennet." Production moved up to the Padana plains in Cremona (where it is still made today) when local milk sources ran out in the early twentieth century. Forget about that rubbery stuff at the local deli. When you want a real provolone, the kind that hangs in a gigantic salami shape from the ceiling, you want Auricchio. It's ideal for shaving over thin slices of carpaccio. Have some Chianti while you're at it.

PROVOLONE, MANDARONE
ITALY | RAW | HARD

This cheese likes to hang around: in Lombardy caves for three years, in the windows of old-world cheese shops. When you taste it, you'll note how the flavor hangs around in your mouth. Raw milk and all that maturity give it an intensely sharp, piquant perfection that will surprise fans of young **provolone**. This classic gourd-shaped, pulled-curd *formaggio* has a thin, shiny rind and straw-colored paste. Used for melting or as a table cheese, it will overpower anything but a robust red wine: Sangiovese, Zinfandel, and the like.

PYRÉNÉES BREBIS

See **Ossau-Ivaty-Brebis Pyrénées**

RACLETTE 🐄

FRANCE AND SWITZERLAND | RAW/PASTEURIZED | WASHED RIND

The famous melter from the ingenious Alpine cheesemakers who once made many a meal by scraping melted cheese off rocks near their smoldering fires. So was born raclette, from the verb *racler*, "to scrape." The semisoft paste is washed during aging, so it's a bit sticky, a bit stinky. The aroma gets pretty fierce as it cooks down, but the flavor is salty and somewhat fruity. Throw a variant of the fondue party: Invite a bunch of friends over, procure a raclette machine (or use your toaster oven), and scrape melted raclette over boiled potatoes, gherkins, and all manner of roasted root vegetables for a hearty winter meal. Avoid cold beverages as the cheese will congeal in your stomach. We like a plummy Merlot blend.

RASCHERA 🐄

ITALY | RAW/PASTEURIZED | SEMISOFT | D.O.P.

From the Maritime Alps come the finest versions of Raschera, made on the Alpaggio (Alpine meadows) from raw milk. Identified by its yellow label, the springy, semisoft cheese is redolent of buttermilk and hay, with a tangy, almond flavor. Down in the valleys, the non-Alpine version is graced with a green label and has a milder, somewhat mushroomy flavor. Both versions are produced exclusively from the milk of Bruno-Alpina or Piemontese cows, though the D.O.P. permits the addition of sheep's or goat's milk. A relatively short aging period, usually capped at three months, means a fresher flavor, though the gray, mold-speckled rind makes for tough chewing. The bright, rich local white, Arneis, is perfectly suited and won't overwhelm.

REBLOCHON

FRANCE | RAW | WASHED RIND | A.O.C.

In medieval times, as a poor, struggling serf, you might work the land from morning till night, only to turn over all your cow's milk to the rich feudal lord, who dominated your life. But suppose one day you only *partially* milked the cows. The second milking, or *reblocher*, was the squeezing of the udder a second time. And by God, the second squeeze was fattier, richer milk. Make a squat patty with that milk, wash it in brine, and you've got serious sustenance in the form of Reblochon.

Each one-pound wheel from the Abondance cow has a smooth, slightly chewy, pink rind and pliant, springy interior. It may bulge, but it's never runny. The flavor is lightly fruity, a bit sour, and satisfyingly eggy. Look for the seal on each wheel of Reblochon: Green means *fermier*, meaning the milk and cheese were produced on a single farm in Savoie. Red means *laitier*, still small production, but the cheesemaker may acquire milk from several local sources. The *fermier* is noticeably stronger in flavor and aroma, with a sticky, ruddy rind and looser, tangier paste that is great with the earthy complexity of red Bordeaux.

RIBAFRIA

PORTUGAL | PASTEURIZED | FIRM

It may look like a regulation hockey puck, but it will taste much better and, though dry and hard, will be easier on the teeth. Hailing from Torres in central Portugal, each flaky round is rolled in coarse black pepper for an aggressive, spicy crust that dominates the flavor of racy goat's milk. This baby is intense and eye-watering, so a sip of sweetness is a prerequisite: Nutty, toasty Madeira keeps the experience appropriately rustic.

RICOTTA

ITALY | PASTEURIZED | FRESH

Literally meaning "recooked," ricotta is made by cooking down the protein-rich whey, the liquid by-product of cheesemaking. Some producers add salt, and if the whey is not from a lactic acid/rennet–precipitated cheese, vinegar can be added to facilitate coagulation. Consisting of water-soluble vitamins, proteins, and minerals, whey is a superfood and after heating offers up delectable proteins that congeal into a cottage cheese–like mass. Most often seen in baked dishes like lasagna, good ricotta deserves an opportunity to impress you straight-up. Enjoy with some unfiltered chestnut honey and a flute of Prosecco for dessert.

RICOTTA SALATA

ITALY | PASTEURIZED | SEMISOFT

Traditional Ricotta Salata is salted, aged sheep's milk ricotta, made from the leftover whey of **Pecorino Romano** production. What you'll find in the United States, however, is essentially a young Pecorino Romano. Traditionally made in Lazio, the snowy, rindless wheels are Italy's answer to feta: pressed, salted, and dried until firm but tender. Milky and salty with a hint of grass, this is an inexpensive option for shaving over tender, peppery spring greens. Try a slab crumbled over juicy cucumbers with a glass of Fumé Blanc.

RIGOTTE

FRANCE | RAW | FRESH

The ancient Roman Empire had great baths, impressive roads, and remarkably good cheese. This squat, rust-colored drum goes back thousands of years. Though its name comes from the Rhône-Alpes dialect for "recooked," Rigotte is not actually produced like ricotta. Instead, it is made from whole milk, and with only a week of aging, it is remarkably creamy and fatty in texture. The annatto dusting on the rind imparts a brighter red hue than brine washing can and is responsible for its slightly sour flavor. The fluffy interior is far more assertive than the diminutive size would suggest. If you're lucky enough to eat one in France, have a glass of local Seyssel. The rest of us can be content with a white Burgundy or another Chardonnay.

RIVER'S EDGE TILLAMOOK BURN

USA | PASTEURIZED | FRESH | VEGETARIAN

When we called cheesemaker Pat Morsford to get some info on the Alpine goats that make the milk for this cheese, we asked, "Do your goats go out on pasture?" To which Pat replied, "They're on the coastal mountain browse." Meaning: These goats wander the craggy, mountainous coast of Oregon, near the Willamette Valley, and eat whatever they please. During the winter, when there is a shortage of nutritious food growing in the damp, foggy air, the goats nosh on dehydrated pumpkin, pumpkin seeds, and grass hay.

With this pristine milk Pat makes the frightening-sounding Tillamook Burn. The name refers to the two-part process of smoking—first of maple leaves and then of leaf-wrapped fresh chèvre—that gives the cheese its signature aroma and flavor. Swathed within the toasty dry leaves is a ball of tangy, milky fresh goat cheese with a windfall of tart, smoky, meaty flavor. Call it the hot dog cheese. Beautiful for cold winter nights with that bottle of Oregon Pinot Noir.

ROBIOLA

ITALY | PASTEURIZED | FRESH

Robiola is Italy's answer to the French tomme, a general moniker given to a diverse range of cheeses—in this case, from Piedmont and Lombardy. Over here, Robiola usually refers to a small, fresh square of cheese. Just this once, we encourage you to think inside the box. Your reward will be a neat cube with a lovely balance of mild, lactic saltiness. It is like the freshest cream cheese you've ever had with no guar gum. Ideal for breakfast, smeared on crusty toast, and mellow enough for your Mimosa.

ROBIOLA BOSINA
ITALY | PASTEURIZED | BLOOMY

This is not *that* Robiola. Sure, it's square and from Piedmont, but bigger and thinner: a luscious slab of creamy, buttery goodness that's all satin on the way down. The addition of sheep's milk gives a bit of tang, and though unlikely to be left uneaten, the insides will run ever so gently across the plate when unattended. It's simple, easy, and pleasing to all, even finicky children, though we do not encourage sharing your Prosecco with the kids.

ROBIOLA DI ROCCAVERANO
ITALY | RAW | FRESH | D.O.P.

Leave it to the Piedmontese to demand stricter regulations and more traditional cheese. This is the only Italian goat's-milk cheese to be bestowed with D.O.P. (name protection), but current regulations allow up to 85 percent cow's milk, which doesn't leave much room for the goats. The finest versions are rarely found here due to their youth, but are nearly all goat's milk, with only a dash of sheep's, meaning that after three weeks of aging, you've got a compact, chalky paste beneath a thin skin smattered with blue mold. Goaty, grassy, and slightly metallic, it goes well with that steely, citrine Gavi.

ROBIOLA ROSSA 🐄 / 🐑

ITALY | RAW | BLOOMY

Take a tender, runny little round of cheese, wrap it in cherry leaves, and you've got this ribbon-bound treat from Piedmont. Don't expect bright, juicy-fruit flavors, but something more akin to the deeply restrained, perfumed musk of flavored tobacco. Woody, dried fruit permeates the otherwise milky, lactic paste, turning an innocuous butterball into something far sexier, in a manly kind of way. The regional grape Nebbiolo, made into Barbaresco, is an ideal partner.

ROBIOLA VITE 🐄 / 🐐 / 🐑

ITALY | RAW | FRESH

Another brilliant leaf-wrapped specimen from Piedmont, featuring all three milks mixed into a moist, cakey round, wrapped in grape leaves and bound with twine. Expect a balance of well-salted milkiness and heady eau-de-vie-type intensity, overlain with the woody depth of bark. Though the cheese is best quite fresh (avoid excessive exterior mold on the leaves or a gushy, runny texture), the leaf binding leaves a flavor imprint of dried grains or tobacco. Its delicacy and surprising complexity are best enjoyed with a quiet white like the local Arneis.

ROCBLEU 🐄

FRANCE | PASTEURIZED | BLUE

Rocbleu is a brand name for the popular style known as "blue **brie**." (Montbriac is another well-known brand name.) Hailing from the Auvergne, it wears a bright blue coat with nothing underneath but buttery spreadability when young. The rind has some moldy, peppery notes, but this is barely a blue. Make a convert of your favorite blue cheese hater, and pair with the flowery aromatics of Fumé (a.k.a. Sauvignon) Blanc.

ROGUE CREAMERY OREGON BLUE VEIN

USA | RAW | BLUE | VEGETARIAN

With more than a half century of cheesemaking history, Rogue Creamery continues to produce this solid, consistent blue under the guidance of Ig Vella, of **Vella Dry Jack** fame. When we can't get the creamery's **Rogue River Blue**, this is the go-to choice. Aged a minimum of ninety days, the creamy, chunky paste sports blue-green striations and surprising nuance. Cheesemaker David Gremmels and his partner Cary Bryant manage to capture a windfall of flavor in each wheel: hints of smoked meat and tangy vegetal tones converge, all in one cheese. They're doing something right in Central Point, Oregon, and local vineyards offer fine Pinot Noir to match.

ROGUE CREAMERY ROGUE RIVER BLUE

USA | RAW | BLUE | VEGETARIAN

Talk about *terroir*! Here is Rogue Creamery's crown jewel, aged for eight months and then wrapped in local grape leaves that have macerated for an entire year in pear eau-de-vie, typical of the region. The two-step process produces a heady, musky fruitiness on the outside and a dense, smoky flavor on the inside. Remember to peel back the leaves and lick your fingers before picking up a snifter of pear eau-de-vie or a dessert white from California.

ROGUE CREAMERY SMOKEY BLUE

USA | RAW | BLUE | VEGETARIAN

Cheesemaker David Grimmels obviously gets his groove on when it comes to blue cheese: his Central Point, Oregon, creamery makes more than half a dozen kinds. Smokey Blue falls into the love-it or hate-it category. Moist, crumbling wheels have a piquant, fruity blue mold flavor but a finishing smoke over hazelnut chips catapults it into cultdom. Think smoldering campfire on a damp autumn evening, and you've got the flavor nailed. We love the balance: you'll still taste that sweet, fresh milk, but the rusticity of smoked meat creeps up on the finish. Find something comparably smoky, like neighboring Pinot Noir for an autumnal joyride.

RONCAL (QUESO RONCAL)

SPAIN | RAW | FIRM | D.O.

Just because it's Spanish sheep's milk doesn't mean it's **Manchego**. In fact, in 1981 Roncal earned the distinction of being the first Spanish cheese awarded D.O. status. Its ancient Navarra origins and production from the milk of Latcha or Aragonese Rasa sheep make Roncal the sister of **Idiazábal**, with a similar rusticity. A musty, waxen rind encases nutty, gamy, barny flavor—lanolin, with notes of warm animal breath, wet wool, and hay. The flaky, pressed paste shaves well; small slivers are perfectly suited to Tempranillo.

ROOMANO

See **Gouda**

ROQUEFORT

FRANCE | RAW | BLUE | A.O.C.

Pliny wrote about it in A.D. 79, and today Roquefort is perhaps the best-known cheese in France, after **Brie**, with a history that is the stuff of fables. So unique are the conditions for Roquefort production that it was the first cheese in France awarded an A.O.C., in 1925. To qualify for esteemed Roquefort status, wheels are produced from Lacaune ewe's milk, held in selected dairies for ten days, and then transported for maturation in the natural caves of Mount Combalou in the commune of Roquefort-sur-Soulzon in southern France. The caves are laced with vertical fissures known as *fleurines*: natural ventilation ducts that maintain a steady 48 degrees (Fahrenheit) and 95 percent humidity.

Amazingly, 60 percent of the Roquefort produced is made by a single company: Société des Caves et des Producteurs Réunis. And most of this 60 percent is sadly mediocre, because good Roquefort is a revelation: clean and assertive but balanced, with a damp, crumbly paste laden with deep pockets of blue. It is rich, peppery, and nutty, with a lingering sweet-salt flavor. The better brands, such as Vieux Berger and Carles, create a wheel that is strong and tangy, rich but not overly salty. The classic pairing is classic for a reason: Sauternes and Roquefort go together like bread and butter.

ROTH KÄSE SOLE GRAN QUESO

USA | PASTEURIZED | FIRM | VEGETARIAN

Break out of your **Manchego** rut via Monroe, Wisconsin. Okay, so this "great cheese" isn't made of sheep milk like Manchego, but it shares that firm, buttery approachability. Aged for six months, these five-pounders maintain a pleasing fleshiness and boast the perfect balance of salt and a long, sweet finish. Great with quince and Marcona almonds if you really want to channel La Mancha, or a generous glass of California Cab to keep it all-American. While it's ideal for groups, it's also compulsively edible enough for picky foodies.

SAINT BLAISE

FRANCE | RAW | WASHED RIND

Come midsummer, the flat grasslands of Provence are dry, sun-crisped, unrelenting. Little shade is offered by scrubby trees dusted in dry, windswept earth. Cows are rare, but goats and sheep pick through gnarled bushes that determine the flavors of their milk. Here, on the border of the Rhône-Alpes, rich sheep's milk is used to make this elegant, aged tomme. The wheels are washed in chicory-infused brine, imparting the husky flavor of bitter greens, well suited to light, chilled rosé.

SAINTE-MAURE-DE-TOURAINE 🐐

FRANCE | RAW | FRESH | A.O.C.

This lovely, lemony log of fresh, goaty goodness is another name-protected hallmark of Loire Valley goat cheese, though most versions on the American market are bland imposters made from pasteurized milk. The defeat of the Arabic Saracens in the town of Sainte-Maure is a pivotal point in the history of Loire Valley goat cheese. Having arrived with both goats and cheese recipes, the Saracens developed what remains to this day the cradle of fresh goat-cheese production. Though they were forced to leave France, their goats (and recipes) remained. A straw runs through each log, promoting airflow and even maturation, all the while infusing the cheese with fresh hayloft aromas. As it ages, expect a firmer, flakier texture beneath a white and blue mold-mottled rind. That creamy ooze just under the rind is piquant, acidic, and walnutty. Loire Valley whites are the natural partner, but a Sauvignon Blanc from California would be lovely, too.

SAINT-FÉLICIEN 🐄

FRANCE | RAW/PASTEURIZED | BLOOMY

Packed in a miniature earthen crock, it is ready to be softened in a warm oven for a few minutes. Scoop up the molten mass of mushroomy paste with slabs of crusty bread. Closely related to **Saint-Marcellin**, this one is creamier, owing to its higher fat content. Made throughout the Rhône-Alpes, the raw milk versions have a deeper complexity and barny tang: savory with a little funk. A local red from the northern Côtes du Rhône emphasizes the spice in that silky paste.

SAINT HANNOIS

FRANCE | RAW | SEMISOFT

A particular local delicacy, Saint Hannois is often carried in the pocket for easy access during mountain strolls through the Rhône-Alpes. This drum is aged to sturdy chewiness with an acidic, fruity lightness. For a mold-covered tidbit, its character is remarkably refreshing—tons of crisp apple and citrus flavors. Seek out the opulence of Viognier or more readily available Sauvignon Blanc.

SAINT-MARCELLIN

FRANCE | RAW/PASTEURIZED | BLOOMY

This crock of cheese is the kid brother to **Saint-Félicien**, though it was originally produced in the Dauphiné region from goat's milk, like a **Banon** without the leaves. These days look for a golden disc in a pottery crock (preferable to plastic, as it's better able to withstand the warmth of an oven). Heating liquefies the satiny cream and concentrates its earthy, truffly flavor. When it is aged for a month, its youthful springiness is relatively mild beneath the thin, bloomy rind. With age, the paste dries and the flavors intensify into robust piquancy. Pair with a spicy Syrah-based red or Châteauneuf-du-Pape.

SAINT-NECTAIRE

FRANCE | RAW/PASTEURIZED | SEMISOFT | A.O.C.

The Salers cows of Auvergne are a busy group, responsible for the raw material of several of

France's finest A.O.C. cheeses. Unfortunately, in this instance, A.O.C. doesn't always mean good cheese. Much of what makes it to market in the United States is industrial, pasteurized Saint-Nectaire, notable for its utterly generic, smooth, pale pink rind and gummy, uninspiring flavor. To find the good stuff, look for the most gnarled rind out there. *Fermier* productions have a thick, uneven brown crust bedecked with patches of yellow, white, and gray mold. To hold a wedge is to breathe damp soil, open fields, and content, ruminating cows. The supple paste is pockmarked with holes and sits heavily on the tongue, dissolving into tangy minerality with whispers of rich, wet straw. A Merlot-dominated Bordeaux, or any Merlot at all, is an elegant match for this complex rusticity.

SAINT-PAULIN

FRANCE | RAW/PASTEURIZED | WASHED RIND

If the ubiquitous cheese Port Salut (a cheese that didn't make this book) had a superior twin, Saint-Paulin would be it. Produced throughout France, but primarily in Normandy, the semisoft wheels are brine washed until a thin, moist rind develops. The flavor is sweet, milky, and mild—approachable and well balanced. It has none of the pasty plasticity of Port Salut, and the rind is a natural orange from that washing, rather than from spray-painted skin. Saint-Paulin has the distinction of being the first French cheese originally produced with pasteurized milk (in 1930). It was not until 1990 that a raw milk version was undertaken. A casual red table wine made from Cabernet Sauvignon works nicely.

SALERS

FRANCE | RAW | FIRM | A.O.C.

The *buron* are small, traditional cheesemaking huts scattered across Auvergne's Massif Central. The Salers are imposing, chestnut-red cows with glorious curved horns. Salers is the sum of these two ancient, traditional parts and, with fewer than five producers remaining, is on the verge of extinction. Strict regulations allow production only between May 1 and October 31, though snow-bound mountains often truncate this production period. After ten months of aging, the wheels have a thick, rocky crust. Beneath, the dense, **Cheddar**-like interior is floral, sour, and gamy. This strong, musty, animal flavor may shock an American palate, but the cheese is worth trying, at least once, for its esteemed history and tradition. Partner with a powerful, full-bodied red. We like the red berry and leather aromas of French Syrah.

SALLY JACKSON CHEESES

USA | RAW | SEMISOFT

One of America's great artisans, Sally Jackson of Okanawa, Washington, said in a recent *Saveur* article, "We don't even get to eat our own cheese, because it's so valuable." And on her extensive cheesemaking training? "I didn't go to France [to learn to make cheese]; I never went to Spain or even Wisconsin . . . I haven't been anywhere. I just milk animals all day." With a small herd of cows, goats, and sheep, Sally makes a triumvirate of semisoft, leaf-wrapped wheels neatly bound in twine. Grape and chestnut leaves (for goat and sheep rounds, respectively) give her cheese a fruity, woody quality that complements the creamy, buttery milk. The springy, compact texture comes from two months' aging. The paste is rich and full, without any runniness. Stay light and local with austere Oregon Pinot Noir.

SALVA CREMASCO

ITALY | PASTEURIZED | SEMISOFT

Save time, save money, save your soul. But save milk? Sure, if you're making cheese in Lombardy. *Salva* means "it saves," and this blocky, crusty square of cheese evolved as a lifeline for dairies with cows producing excessive amounts of milk in early spring. Make a bigger wheel that can age for longer, and you've got something to sell (and eat) come fall. Beneath its gnarled, nut-colored rind, Salva has a crumbling, white paste. Brine washing early in its life delivers an underlying funk. The earthy aroma of wet autumn leaves develops with age. Think of it as a drier, aged **Taleggio**, and get a white from northern Italy, like Pinot Blanc or Pinot Gris.

SAVAL

WALES | RAW | WASHED RIND | VEGETARIAN

This variant on Welsh Celtic Promise is, we promise you, bigger and better. So many English and Welsh cheeses are firm **Cheddar** types that it's often hard for us colonials to differentiate among them. From cheesemaker James Aldridge comes this notable exception. Young cheese is smeared with hard cider to create a softer, damper wheel with a lovely, sticky, spicy rind. More delicate than its Irish counterparts, such as **Durrus**, and heartier than the French **Epoisses** types, Saval is perfectly suited to a glug of cider, like Ciderjack.

SCAMORZA
ITALY | PASTEURIZED | SEMISOFT

A tiny shrunken head of a cheese, Scamorza gets its name from the southern Italian colloquialism meaning "beheaded." Traditionally the head takes on many guises, especially at Easter, when it is molded into the shapes of little rabbits, chicks, you name it. Aged longer than other *pasta filata* types, like **mozzarella**, this cheese has a semifirm and elastic texture; the rind is smooth, oily, and lightly caramel-colored. It is made in the Italian province of Bari and is used in a local traditional dish called *quagghiaridde*, a combination of mutton, Scamorza, eggs, and salami that is baked and served with boiled arugula. Look for the bigger red wines of southern Italy alongside the salty, chewy, straw-colored paste of the cheese, baked or enjoyed alone.

SECHONS DE L'ISERE
FRANCE | RAW | FIRM

It's not often we're excited when a cheese looks like a moldy, dried-out, old disc of **Saint-Marcellin**, but here's the exception. The distinctly fruity aroma, like Concord grapes and fresh yeasty bread, plays off background goaty smells. The texture is neither crumbly nor flaky, but breaks into chunks that dissolve delightfully on the tongue.

The flavor is complex, with strong tropical fruit flavors of mango and pineapple. This cheese produces a pleasant burn on the front of the tongue; Chardonnay will help prolong the experience.

SELLES-SUR-CHER

FRANCE | RAW | FRESH | A.O.C.

From Loire-sur-Cher comes Selles-sur-Cher, one of the best-known ashed goat cheeses in France. Creamy, fresh rounds were traditionally dusted in wood ash to encourage the development of a mold rind, aglow with patches of blue, green, and gray. These days powdered charcoal is used. As the paste ages and sheds moisture, it tightens and the flavors intensify: tart, briny, mouth-sticking wet clay, all wreathed in whiffs of fresh milk and new-mown grass. This cheese is known for its compatibility with Sauvignon Blanc from France, California, or South Africa.

SERPA

PORTUGAL | RAW | SEMISOFT | VEGETARIAN | D.O.P.

Both Spain and Portugal produce a wonderful yet motley crew of *amanteigado* cheeses: succulent wheels with guts of pudding and varying degrees of sour, vegetal intensity. Serpa is the moderate one: more assertive than **Amarelo de Beiva Baixa**, but lacking the outstanding finesse of **Serra da Estrella**. Made with the milk of Merino sheep and coagulated with thistle, this little lamb is floral and fatty with high acidic notes that can be eaten soupy or semisoft. Portuguese Vinho Verde flies alongside.

SERRA DA ESTRELA

PORTUGAL | RAW | SEMISOFT | VEGETARIAN | D.O.P.

Made for centuries in the mountains of the Serra da Estrela range with the milk of Bordaleira sheep, this is the king of Portuguese cheese. Neatly bound in strips of soft cotton, runny young wheels drip with the butterfat of farmhouse sheep's milk. That cardoon thistle coagulant is present in the bright, fresh, floral flavor. The firmer aged version is stronger, cleanly sliceable, with the beginning insistence of caramel on the finish. This revered old monarch needs wine with depth and nuance: reds from Bordeaux and Rioja are highly recommended.

SERRAT DEL TRIADÓ

SPAIN | RAW | HARD

You take a classic Spanish cheese name and modify it, and things get confusing. In this case, Serrat refers to a smooth sheep's-milk cheese originating in the Catalan Pyrénées. *Serrat* means "tight": no holes, no fissures, no wrinkles, nothing. Which is great, except our Serrat (del Triadó) is a pressed cow's-milk cheese aged from four months to one year. Using the milk from a small collective of five farmers, production is overseen by Spain's foremost *queso* expert: Enric Canut. Hard cow's-milk cheese is unusual in a region devoted to sheep, and its assertive, almost biting sharpness has a long, burning finish that is easily tempered with a glass of Tempranillo.

SHARPHAM RUSTIC

ENGLAND | PASTEURIZED | SEMISOFT | VEGETARIAN

Triple-crèmes are all cream-enriched, buttery pastes. But what happens if you enrich your milk with cream and then age it? Devon cheesemaker Debbie Mumford's Sharpham Rustic is an impressive, dusty-white flying saucer with a remarkably rich, golden, semifirm paste, thanks to unctuous Devon cream. Also look for the herb version, inspired by cows grazing on wild garlic, which produces a chivey, onion-laced flavor. The herd of seventy Jersey cows enjoys life on organic pastures, part of a five-hundred-acre compound owned by the Sharpham Trust. A hearty nut-brown ale will offset the richness.

SHROPSHIRE BLUE

ENGLAND | PASTEURIZED | BLUE | VEGETARIAN

Created by Mrs. Hutchison Smith in the 1970s, Shropshire demands acknowledgment. It's as if staid **Stilton** had a more flamboyant twin. From beneath a dusty, natural rind, the annatto-infused, crocus-yellow paste shines forth, mapped with rivulets of blue-green mold. This dense and fudgy wheel hails from Nottinghamshire, and it's moderately salted, with Stilton's approachable, mellow flavor. The paste is more mineral than tongue-tickling spice and pairs perfectly with port.

SLACK MA GIRDLE

ENGLAND | PASTEURIZED | WASHED RIND | VEGETARIAN

You'll snap your girdle upon tasting this English upstart. Named for a cider apple native to England's midcountry, this cheese is soft, sticky, and green as Kermit the Frog, and in no way incorporates said apple into its rind or paste. Instead, the semisoft wheels are coated with dried nettle leaves, imparting a mild, lemony flavor somewhere between parsley and thyme. Give a nod to the apples; have some hard cider from Woodchuck or Ciderjack, or a glass of lemony Sauvignon Blanc.

SONOMA CHEESE FACTORY SONOMA JACK

USA | PASTEURIZED | SEMISOFT

An American original first made in Monterey, California, Jack opened this great country up to a world of gooey omelets, nachos, and cheese fries. The smooth, rindless wheels have a lactic, tangy, fresh-milk taste and, needless to say, melt wonderfully. Sonoma Cheese Factory, a third-generation family business, was the first cheese factory west of the Mississippi to win a gold medal in Wisconsin. Originally begun in 1931 as a partnership between Celso Viviani and the Vella family, Sonoma Cheese Factory is now run by Celso's son, Pete, and grandson, David. Popular variants of the cheese are laced with shavings of hot pepper. This isn't a wine cheese; it's a cooking one, useful in anything requiring some melting pizzazz. Okay, you won't die if you sip an equally lush California Chardonnay alongside a wedge.

SOTTOCENERE

ITALY | PASTEURIZED | SEMISOFT

Laborious to make, easy to eat. Hefty wheels studded with slivers of black truffle are rubbed in ash (*Sottocenere* means "under the ashes") and aromatic ground spices, including nutmeg, coriander, cinnamon, licorice, cloves, and fennel. It's a heady, aromatic coat for this delicate, silky-smooth cheese from the Veneto. The truffle is merely one note in the symphony, so if you're seeking musky, sexy truffle overload, look instead to **Pecorino Tartufello**. With a flute of dry Lambrusco and dried red fruits, however, expect a full spectrum of sensuality.

SOUMAINTRAIN

FRANCE | RAW/PASTEURIZED | WASHED RIND

This bigger **Epoisses** type from Burgundy, with a sunken, viscous rind and powerful barnyard aromas, is likely to challenge neophytes. The larger format can withstand longer aging, but with added time comes greater intensity. You get a thick pudding with salt and cream, but also spice and the burn of high-alcohol Marc de Bourgogne, with which it's liberally doused. Try a glass of Alsatian Riesling, regional partner to comparably assertive **Munster**.

SPROUT CREEK TOUSSAINT

USA | RAW | FIRM | VEGETARIAN

Up in Poughkeepsie, New York, there's a farm run by nuns who have created something like farmhouse **Cheddar** crossed with a heady **Tomme de Savoie**. The dense, crumbly, honey-yellow paste is protected by a thick, rocky crust with powerful damp-cave aromas. The taste is sharp but deeply buttery, rich, and lingering, with full grassiness and the beginnings of butterscotch. Their other cheeses, Ouray and Barat, are available in smaller sizes than the ten-pound Toussaint. In fact, the Barat is noteworthy for its tiny size (eight ounces), as well as its quick ripening and butterscotchy aged **Gouda** flavors. All are well suited to a carafe of something rough and dry, like Chianti.

STANSER FLADÄ

SWITZERLAND | RAW | WASHED RIND

Every country must have a cheese named for dung, and this is Switzerland's contribution, as well as one of the country's best offerings. *Fladä* means "patty," and if you sit in a closed room with this cheese, the reason becomes apparent. A relatively new cheese created to meet the year-round demand for **Vacherin Mont d'Or** (available only during the winter months), Stanser Fladä is a ripe, round patty tucked into a wooden box. The reddish-brown crust can be broken with a spoon to steal a bit of the thick, runny insides, with their strong, earthen, petrol flavor. This cheese is assertive, so a soft Viognier (or other Chenin Blanc) is best.

STANSER RÖTELI

SWITZERLAND | RAW | WASHED RIND

"The little red one from Stans" comes from the namesake town nestled near Lake Lucerne in central Switzerland. Joseph Barmettler uses milk from the small herds of five farmers whose animals feast in the mountains, just below the alpage. The red rind blossoms after diligent brine washing, digesting the paste until the wheels are limp and thick as warm peanut butter. Strong, full, and biting, with a dash of sweat, it's positively acrid when overripe. We need something oily and sweet, Sauternes or other viscous dessert whites, to add some elegance to this barnyard brashness.

STANSER SCHAFCHÄS

SWITZERLAND | RAW | WASHED RIND

Another stinker from Stans, the Swiss town near the star-shaped Lake Lucerne. Cheesemaker Joseph Barmettler must have a tolerant sense of smell. This one is "the sheep cheese from Stans," and so great is its prominence it needs no more specific name. Firmer than **Stanser Röteli**, it hits you with sharp, jabbing aromas of peat moss, like damp, fermented soil. Despite this opener, the interior paste is remarkably mellow and very vegetal, even fruity, like the Portuguese thistle cheeses. You could melt it on potatoes or find a bottle of Pinot Blanc that can stand up to the competition.

STILLTON

ENGLAND | PASTEURIZED | BLUE | VEGETARIAN (IN ALL CASES EXCEPT SOME BY COLSTON BASSETT)

The only English cheese protected by legislation, Stilton is probably the best-known blue in the world. It has been produced since 1720, when one cheesemaker (Nottinghamshire's Elizabeth Scarbrow, followed by her daughter and granddaughter) maintained a corner on the market for fifty years. By 1790, the good thing had caught on, and every village nearby was cranking it out.

A good production (and don't be fooled; there are many more mediocre Stiltons than there are good ones) is an impeccable marriage of a heavy, moist paste, sparkling minerality, balanced salt, and roasted nuttiness. Unlike most blue cheeses, which are pierced within a week of production to encourage blueing, Stilton ages for an entire month and is then pierced as many as three hundred times. The large cylindrical wheels have, by this point, developed a rough-hewn, sandy crust that imbues the cheese with earthy nuance. Three producers stand out above all the rest: Colston Bassett, Cropwell Bishop, and Long Clawson. Serve with tawny port and that's that. There are no other options.

STINKING BISHOP

ENGLAND | PASTEURIZED | WASHED RIND | VEGETARIAN

The name refers to a type of pear, not to an unwashed clergyman, alas. This puddle of cheese made by Charles Martell in Gloucestershire is washed in perry, a hard cider made from pears, before it is bound in a springy strip of beechwood. We serve it in a dish; you'll need to, because no plate can contain this steadily spreading mass. Heady, fruity, and all thick milkiness, the Bishop pairs well with a dry, lightly effervescent hard cider.

STRACCHINO

ITALY | PASTEURIZED | FRESH

Traditionally, Stracchino was produced in autumn from the milk of cows journeying from the high summer pastures of Lombardy to their winter abodes in the valleys. Having lumbered for miles, the cows were *stracca*, or tired, and the milk they gave was especially full of complex and varied flavors from months of summer grazing on delicate flowers and wild herbs. This milk was cloth drained and ripened on mats for several days, then the cheese was eaten fresh: soft, tart, and lactic beneath a thin, nearly translucent skin. These days production is almost entirely industrial, and though you may still find raw milk versions from tiny local producers, we're not this lucky here at home. Look also for **Crescenza**, a member of the Stracchino family, which is made throughout the Po River valley, always from pasteurized milk; it has a milder, more delicate flavor and fresh-milk aroma. Drizzled with honey, either version is lovely for a light dessert, alongside a sip of Moscato d'Asti.

SUAU DE CLUAU (QUESO DEL MONTSEC)

SPAIN | PASTEURIZED | SEMISOFT

Most cheeses from the Basque region have a rough edge, and the sheep's-milk cheeses are decidedly rustic. The locals prefer a flavor that's "hot": gamy and meaty, like lamb chops. This sweet little wheel is an exception to the rule: The firm but unctuous paste is delicate, with aromas of mushroom and wet stone offsetting a sour finish that carries on for several minutes. The unusual mustiness makes us reach for the rich, toasty, oxidized flavors of white Rioja.

TALEGGIO

ITALY | PASTEURIZED | WASHED RIND | D.O.P.

Welcome to Stinky Cheese 101, where we learn that despite pungent, nearly offensive aromas, flavors can be gentle, buttery, and mild. The lush rolling grasslands of Lombardy are the source of great milk, transmogrified into this meaty, salty square with the compulsively edible yeastiness of freshly baked bread. If that sunny, cantaloupe-colored rind is overly gray and furry, things have gotten out of hand, though the smell of ammonia will tip you off if your eyes do not. For Italy's answer to barny greats like **Epoisses de Bourgogne**, find a crisp, neutral white like Pinot Grigio and convert a cheese newbie today.

TARENTAIS

FRANCE | RAW | WASHED RIND

Hailing from the eponymous region in Savoie, this one is for connoisseurs of goat cheese. Liberal washing in the local white wine Seyssel gives a raisiny, fruity flavor and a peachy rind that ages to maraschino-cherry pink (think terrible-teen hair dye). This little nugget is in it for the long haul, aging an astounding sixty to ninety days to refined, powder-crumble perfection. Rarely found in the United States, it goes well with a lush white like Chenin Blanc.

TAYLOR FARM SMOKED GOUDA

USA | RAW | SEMISOFT

A few years ago we would've sneered, "Smoked Gouda? Try the supermarket." And then Jon Wright of Londonderry, Vermont, came along with this husky lad. All good cheese deserves a chance, and this is the best smoked Gouda we've ever tasted. Vermonters are a hearty bunch—ice fishing, sugaring, running around in the snow— they need a hearty cheese. This is one you can sink your teeth into, heady with real smoke (not some Liqui-junk in a bottle), like a wedge of wet autumn. For cheese guys, there's always the need for the perfect nosh on Super Bowl Sunday, on poker night, or while waiting for dinner. As comfy with Newcastle as a drunk guy in a jersey.

TELEME

USA | PASTEURIZED | SEMISOFT

From California's Peluso Creamery, here is an American original with eighty years of cheesemaking history. Fat, soft, bone-colored squares are dusted in rice flour and can be sold young, when the flavor is tart and mild—comparable to (but better than) fresh Jack-type cheeses. Melt it down over nachos or eggs for some gooey oomph. After two to three months, however, nature has done the melting for you, and the square becomes a dangerously jiggling mass: pungent, meaty, and scoopable. This is when it gets interesting, especially over a few bottles of California Merlot.

TÊTE DE MOINE

SWITZERLAND | RAW | FIRM

If you have a *girolle*, a nifty little machine designed for the sole purpose of shaving paper-thin slices of this "monk's head," you can create artistic flowers of melting, toffee-colored richness. The name refers to a one-cheese-per-year tax paid by Swiss monks to the prior of the Abbey of Bellelay in Switzerland. This firm, supple-pasted cylinder is a winter favorite, with a fierce aroma and gently spicy, nutty flavor. We like to shave the monk with a group of friends, preferably sharing a vat of mulled wine.

TETILLA (QUESO DE TETILLA)

SPAIN | PASTEURIZED | SEMISOFT | D.O.

It doesn't take much imagination to guess that *Tetilla* means "tit," and sure enough, each two-pounder looks like a hefty, if somewhat artificial, breast. The Galicians regularly enjoy this springy, elastic lovely as a classic table cheese—buttery, tart, and milky. The thick rind is not great for eating, but the mild, creamy paste inside is. And it's perfect for melting, alongside a carafe of Albariño.

THISTLE HILL TARENTAISE

USA | RAW | FIRM

No, the cheese isn't jaundiced. That neon-yellow hue comes from milk so rich in beta-carotene it practically glows. Vermonters John and Janice Putnam set out to re-create the windfall of flavor they loved in French **Beaufort**. The cooked, pressed flesh is made from the milk of twenty or so Jersey cows, in a two-hundred-year-old, 850-liter copper kettle imported from Switzerland. That smooth paste is peppered with tiny pockmarks, and infinitely layered with nutty flavor and a sly, spicy finish that creeps up after you swallow. But careful aging also unveils toast, scalded cream, and fruity flavors that blow us away. Our specially aged wheels (around fourteen months) are rich with a candied-pineapple finish that melds beautifully with fruity, full-on reds of the Super Tuscan sort.

TICKLEMORE

ENGLAND | PASTEURIZED | SEMISOFT | VEGETARIAN

Once upon a time, Robin Congdon's powdery white orb known as Ticklemore was made of raw milk, with a flood of lactic, fungal flavor. These days it's pasteurized, and though it retains the moist, curdy paste we love for its squeak across the teeth, it's a bit milder, but still milky and satisfying, with a heady wet-clay aroma. Watch the moisture level, though. If it gets too damp it becomes a sodden, muddy mess. Long before it ever reaches this point, eat it up with luscious Italian Soave.

TOLEDO

PORTUGAL | PASTEURIZED | FIRM

We're talking Estremadura, Portugal, not Ohio. The gussied-up russet rind should tip you off: You're not in the United States anymore. Produced just north of Lisbon, this cheese is made of three milks mixed into a solid puck that is aged and smeared with paprika. Though firm, the paste is creamy, kissed with the peppery smoke of good chorizo. A full, fruity Tempranillo is a good Iberian choice.

TOMME CRAYEUSE

FRANCE | RAW | SEMISOFT

This chalky tomme could be just another **Tomme de Savoie** wannabe. Produced in Savoie, it's got that dank, mold-dappled rind and the same mountain-fed cow's milk, but two stages of aging catapult it into mushroomy epiphany. First, it lounges in the cave, warm and saturated with humidity to loosen the flesh into marshmallow cream. Then, a visit to a cooler but equally moist cave teases out those earthy, lactic inclinations, preserving an inner core of milky crumble. The final wheel is pure mushroom butter with a smattering of gorgeous powdery yellow mold, the result of cellulose in the cows' diet. The intense richness of flavor is deflected by a spicy red Syrah.

TOMME DE LA CHATAIGNERAIE

FRANCE | RAW | SEMISOFT

Goats are troupers. They'll go anywhere and eat anything, though we've yet to catch one munching a tin can. The Auvergne goats responsible for this tomme eat their way through chestnut tree groves (*chataigneraie*), enjoying sticks and sprigs, nuts and leaves, and whatever grows in between. No wonder the thick, mottled rind and supple, meaty paste are the essence of roasted chestnut. As if all that fodder weren't enough, the wheels are then aged on chestnut planks. For all that work, you get a rustic paste that manages to be roasted-nut rich and delicate at the same time. Unlike fresher styles, the long aging time on these big wheels means they are available (and delicious) all year round. We like a white wine with a bit of funk to it; if you can find Loire Savennières, you'll be in goat heaven.

TOMME DE L'ARIÈGE

FRANCE | RAW | WASHED RIND

In the Midi-Pyrénées town of Loubière, one cheesemaker is mixing things up. He bases his recipe on **Reblochon**, but ages the wheels for several months in damp, dark caves. This musty, brine-washed tomme reaches the apex of goaty greatness from November to January. That's it. Earlier in the season when the paste is gummy and unyielding, the flavor is shallow and slightly sour. But for those two months, when the insides are runny and sweet, this is one of the finest goat cheeses in the world, with the color of carrots and the flavor of hazelnuts. A Kabinett Riesling is our choice at any time.

TOMME DE LOUBIÈRE

FRANCE | RAW | SEMISOFT

This tomme is cushiony enough to lay your tired head on, except it's painted with charcoal, so you'd wake up smeared with viscous black ash. For similar reasons, the rind is not great for eating, but we like the inside because the flavor and texture are so weird. Springy and elastic, the paste slithers and slips across your tongue, big and winey with a pronounced bitter almond finish.

Produced in the Midi-Pyrénées, across the valley from **Tomme de l'Ariège**, it's another exceptional trailblazer, aged for two to three months, and best softened with a bright Pinot Blanc.

TOMME DE SAVOIE 🐄
FRANCE | RAW/PASTEURIZED | SEMISOFT

This defining tomme comes in many guises, raw and pasteurized, whole milk and skimmed, industrial and *fermier* production. It's hard to know what you're getting when you order a "round from Savoie." So we'll tell you what to look for: a knobby, russet-colored rind, pitted, with a smattering of yellow and white mold. Inside, the paste should be toothsome but sticky, riddled with tiny holes, straw-blond, and melting on the tongue. Without visual cues, rely on your nose alone: damp cellar, wet straw, mown grass, and a hint of ammonia (that's right, a hint is a normal and natural part of this rustic, heavy-rinded wheel). More than a whiff and the tomme is done. The flavor is savory and buttery, though the finish can pack a mouthwatering punch in peak season. Bold reds from the Rhône-Alpes are appropriate.

TOMME DES TEMPLIERS 🐐
FRANCE | RAW | SEMISOFT

The Knights Templar searched for the Holy Grail, and this grail of goatiness is stamped to this day with the identifying mark of the Occitan cross from southwestern France. Four months in a cave on damp planks imparts a musty woodiness. This is serious cheese, made by a single producer in the Midi-Pyrénées, around the bend from Tomme de l'Ariège and Tomme de Loubière. True believers know enough to snag some dry Chardonnay before heading out on any quest.

TOMME DU BERGER

FRANCE | RAW | WASHED RIND

"Wheel of the shepherd" means this Provençal cheesemaker adjusts his recipe depending on available quantities of milk. What we like about the changing face of Tomme du Berger is its tightrope walk between barny and mellow. Wicker basket imprints leave the rind crosshatched. The sticky rind barely contains a bulging, intensely fatty paste, thanks to the work of diligent sheep. For all its buttery richness, salty assertion, and animal aromas, the cheese is mercurial, as it is often remarkably fruity, with ripe pear flavors. Taste throughout the year with crisp whites or soft reds, from white Côtes du Rhône to Beaujolais.

TOMMETTE DE LUCCIANA

FRANCE | RAW | SEMISOFT

This sweet little patty is cloaked in the self-important rind of a mountain tomme: knobby with a dusting of rust, yellow, and gray molds; each thin diskette from Corsica is a half inch of rich, fatty paste. It offers the bounty of lightly aged sheep's milk: grassy, herbaceous, and kissed by the earthiness of that ridged rind. We like it with an elegant Pinot Noir from Burgundy, ideally, to pay homage to the cheese's balance and heft.

TOMMETTE DES ALPES

FRANCE | RAW | SEMISOFT

"Little tomme from the Alpes," your squat round-ness is like larger, better-known tommes, as is your mold-mottled rind. But where the bigger, older tommes are dusty brown and earthen, you retain a light, fresh succulence. Shorter maturation preserves your creamy, supple, mushroomy paste. Your mixture of milks was introduced to maintain production during those months when milk in the Haute-Savoie was scarce; the combi-nation gives you a rich, aromatic complexity well suited to a light white like Pinot Grigio.

TOMMETTE MORGÉE AU SEYSSEL

FRANCE | RAW | WASHED RIND

Seyssel makes another appearance, here wash-ing the thin "little tomme" from the Rhône-Alpes. For **Tarentais** and **Le Valleroger**, a wine bath im-parts raisiny sweetness, but for Morgée the result is entirely savory, not unlike razor-thin slices of pro-sciutto: sweet and hammy, with a luscious, melting texture. The rind can be thick and chewy, even a bit gritty, but the bulging meatiness inside is worth carving out. A rich, succulent white like Gewürz-traminer works well.-

TOMME VAUDOISE

SWITZERLAND | RAW | BLOOMY

A little tomme, like the **Camembert** of your fan-tasies. Beneath a papery rind of soft bloom you will find the soupy essence of freshly drawn milk, mushrooms, and a bit of cream. So delicate is this patty from the Vaud that aging for even twenty-four hours too long can turn its subtle earthiness to smelly barnyard. A prickly, yeasty Champagne carries the earthiness for long, indulgent minutes.

TORTA DEL CASAR (QUESO TORTA DEL CASAR)

SPAIN | RAW | SEMISOFT | VEGETARIAN | D.O.

A mind-blowing three-pounder from Extremadura is meant to be served with the top sliced off and the puddinglike innards scooped up with chorizo. This one is coagulated with cardoon thistle, and the piquant, floral flavor is similar to that of **La Serena**, but kicked up a notch. It's unctuous, with a pronounced sourness that can border on astringent, thanks to the provocative milk of the Churra sheep; we find it a little woody, like freshly stripped bark. The flavor is particular, but its wine versatility is not: good with a range from light, crisp whites (Sauvignon Blanc) to heady Rhône reds.

UBRIACO AL PROSECCO

ITALY | RAW/PASTEURIZED | FIRM

It doesn't actually mean "drunk in disguise," but compared with **Ubriaco Gran Riserva**, it's the less obvious of the two drunken Italian cheeses. With no glowing purple rind to betray its wine infusion, you might think Ubriaco al Prosecco had never touched the stuff; however, it's had its share of the grape. This time, the rind has been washed with Prosecco, making for a golden, pale exterior and a fruity, winey tang. The delicate, sunny sweetness is the ideal bite for summertime along with a chilled glass of sparkling Prosecco.

UBRIACO GRAN RISERVA
ITALY | RAW/PASTEURIZED | FIRM

Many things sound better when spoken in Italian. The name of this cheese is a fine example, since it basically means "great big drunk." This firm, crumbly wheel is smeared with the musts of Cabernet, Merlot, and Reboso wines, giving it a mouth-puckering fermented grapiness. Look closely at the deep violet rind—there are often fossilized speckles of grape seeds and sticks, reminding you that this is one of those products that could never be made in a factory. It's a cheese that's hard not to love, especially alongside a tumbler of Barbaresco.

UPLANDS CHEESE COMPANY PLEASANT RIDGE RESERVE (EXTRA AGED)
USA | RAW | FIRM

This excellent Alpine-inspired cheese is controlled from milk to wheels by Mike and Carol Gingrich and their partners Dan and Jeanne Patenaude in Dodgeville, Wisconsin. Dan oversees the herd of mixed-breed cows, while Mike makes this superlative cheese from a modified **Beaufort** recipe. Here is definitive proof that American cheese need not be flaccid and plasticky. The American Cheese Society agreed, awarding it Best in Show in 2001 and 2005. Rich with flavors of dried plum and apricot, olive and savory, it rivals the best French and Swiss mountain cheeses. This smooth, brilliant wheel is aged at least nine months, when sporadic amino acid crystals begin to appear; at fourteen months, it becomes more intensely butterscotchy, approaching Dutch **Roomano**, but without the bitterness—this extra age is worth the extra money. Savor, and slowly sip a ripe, spicy Cahors.

VACHERIN FRIBOURGEOIS

SWITZERLAND | RAW/PASTEURIZED | SEMISOFT

Wet earth, well-trod grass, and scalded milk are all captured in a heady perfume that is Vacherin Fribourgeois. This is no hard, nutty mountain cheese, but a dense, sensual, melting pâte produced in the canton of Fribourg and other parts of western Switzerland. We have only to unwrap a wheel to imagine the Alpine pastures of its origin. Most Swiss dairies have given up on the raw milk version, making its moist, popcorn-buttery, complex flavor all the more precious. A lush, fruity Chardonnay smooths that dirt-under-the-nails rusticity.

VACHERIN MONT D'OR

SWITZERLAND | RAW/PASTEURIZED | WASHED RIND

We're often asked, "What is the world's best cheese?" We have many favorites, but this highly seasonal delicacy may be the greatest of all cheeses. It's available for a few fleeting winter months, and the similar French cheese, Vacherin du Haut-Doubs, is protected by A.O.C. regulations that state the cheese cannot be made from the milk of cows fed silage or fermented fodder. The animals may be inside, but they can't have anything other than sweet, dry hay.

The responsibility for the origin of this luscious delicacy was a matter of some contention, with both France and Switzerland claiming ownership for the cheese made on both sides of the Massif du Mont d'Or. France has been producing it for two centuries, and eventually Switzerland conceded invention. We're telling you about the Swiss version for two reasons. First, this is the name it goes by in the states, regardless of origin. More importantly, the Swiss version can be pasteurized, and is therefore legal in the U.S. The French version must, by A.O.C. law, be raw milk.

The runny ooze is contained by a wooden box, and though the blushing puddle seems formidable, the flavor is intensely milky, barely sharp, delicately woodsy. The best wheels are spoonable, a bit spicy, simply luscious, commanding exuberance, especially with a spicy Gewürztraminer.

VALDEÓN

SPAIN | PASTEURIZED | BLUE

In a case of mistaken identity, this mixed-milk cheese is often confused with **Cabrales**, a far more assertive cheese, though it lacks the signature sycamore leaf wrapping. Valdeón has a moist, marbled, blue-veined interior and relatively mellow sweetness. Its leathery, earthy undertones are delicious, but markedly softer and gentler than the spicy ferocity of Cabrales. Make a toast to Spain with Oloroso sherry.

VALENÇAY

FRANCE | RAW | FRESH | A.O.C.

The story goes that Valençay was once an elegant, regal, pointy pyramid, dusted in fine black charcoal. Then Napoleon, on his return from an utterly failed campaign to conquer Egypt, caught sight of this stately pyramid and was so enraged that he drew his sword and lopped off its top. Reduced to a squat trapezoid, Valençay posed less of a threat to the little man's ego, and he continued on his journey. Or so goes the story. To this day, the shape remains truncated, but the moist, heavy paste is full and melting, with sweet hay aromas and a slightly sour crumble on the tongue. Beware imposters: The real specimen is unpasteurized. A dry Sauvignon Blanc softens the goaty tang.

VARE (QUESO VARE)

SPAIN | PASTEURIZED | FIRM

On the coast of Spain's northern Asturias, a clean, grassy wedge of cheese is Vare-y refreshing. Say you don't like goat cheese? We say: Try this on for size. A month of aging sheds moisture and typical tang, leaving a firm, smooth-rinded round smelling of cool, damp caves. The mild, grassy flavor is simple and direct, a beautiful introduction to goat cheese, without a trace of barn. Find an elegant, grassy white like Albariño for quiet companionship.

VELLA DRY JACK

USA | RAW | HARD | VEGETARIAN

Beginning in 1931, the Vella family produced California Jack cheese from raw milk but aged it longer than other makers to appeal to the growing population of Italian immigrants who knew hard grating cheese like **Grana Padano**. In the Italian tradition of the time, the wheels were smeared with lampblack. These days, Ig Vella of Sonoma, California, continues to produce hard, dry wheels with a flaking, straw-colored paste. It's nutty, yes, but also sweet like caramel, with crunch. We must note that a thick outer coating of cocoa powder is a vast improvement on lamp residue, adding a bittersweet chocolate note that is well suited to California Cabernet.

VENTO D'ESTATE OR

ITALY | PASTEURIZED | FIRM

One of our favorite new finds. Wrapped in strands of green-golden straw smelling of summer, the complex, nubbly paste is sharp but sweet, as though washed in opulent white wine. And the rest is all pesto: great handfuls of freshly torn basil, peppery and rich. Made of sheep's or cow's milk, these wheels of summer are light, vegetal, delightful. Any of the slinky whites from northern Italy, like Pinot Blanc, work with this Valtellina jewel.

WEINKASE

SWITZERLAND | RAW | SEMISOFT

This seasonal cheese is made during the vineyard harvest in eastern Switzerland, where buttercup-yellow cow's milk from happy beasts gorged on the grasses of pine meadows is molded into a moist, supple patty and rubbed down with dank, black grape must. Unlike the Italian versions, all peppy fruit, this one is more challenging: husky with the pungent smells of leather and alcohol. The buttery paste retains the nippy flavor of fermented grape. For this aggressive cheese, try a round, caramelized Chardonnay from California.

WESTFIELD CAPRI

USA | PASTEURIZED | FRESH | VEGETARIAN

Fresh chèvre relies on immediate production and close proximity to market to retain its vibrant, creamy, tangy character. Westfield Farm has both, producing cheese several times a week, only a few hours away from Murray's. The lactic, milky paste has a delicate character with citrusy flavors and none of the graininess that can mar fresh, rindless goat cheese. An ideal starter on a cheese plate, it has a clean finish that leaves no residual flavors. Supreme with goat's natural partner, Sauvignon Blanc, we like to stay American with the richer versions from California.

WESTFIELD CLASSIC BLUE LOG

USA | PASTEURIZED | FRESH | VEGETARIAN

That small, aquamarine log in the Murray's counter looks like blue cheese, but you cut it open and see fluffy, snowy paste and think "goat cheese." So, which is it? Well, this little log from the farm of Bob and Debby Stetson in Hubbardston, Massachusetts, has a bit of an identity crisis, because it's both. The brilliant blue mold is mixed into the milk during cheesemaking, as with any blue cheese.

But the log is never pierced. The mold inside is never in contact with oxygen. The mold never grows. So instead of spicy blue, you get cakey, tart fresh goat cheese: a surprise for your nerdy cheese friends and lovely for the dog days of summer. It's delightful with a Chenin Blanc, which, like us, enjoys both blues and goats.

WILLOW HILL SUMMER TOMME
USA | PASTEURIZED | VEGETARIAN

Willow Smart's done a take on one of our favorite European choices: the herb-encrusted slab known as **Brin d'Amour** or **Fleur du Maquis**. It happily reminds us of the slightly sour, refreshing, semisoft, poetically named cheeses from Corsica. Liberally coated with a selection of northern Vermont herbs, including rosemary, thyme, savory, and lavender, it's like eating a wedge of moist, savory cake. The perfect balance of salt, cream, and warm, sunny rosemary, it is complemented by the roundness of California Fume Blanc.

ZAMORANO (QUESO ZAMORANO)
SPAIN | RAW | FIRM | D.O.

More so even than **Roncal**, Zamorano runs the risk of confusion with **Manchego**. It's got the same crosshatch on the rind, the same firm, fine, straw-colored paste. But the similarities end there. Made from the thick milk of Churra and Castilian sheep in northwestern Castilla y León, these wheels age to incredible fullness. Dry, sharp, with a hint of butterscotch that recalls well-aged **Gouda**, the sweet crunch is especially well suited to velvety Ribera del Duero.

ACCOMPANIMENTS FOR CHEESE

One of the most frequently asked questions we get at Murray's is, "What do I serve with cheese?" When we're considering what to eat with cheese, we think about contrasting textures and flavors: salty with sweet, spicy with sour, creamy with crunchy. Before a meal we prefer fresh flavors (see the following suggestions) or small chunks of aged, salty cheese (like Parmigiano-Reggiano) with a bit of ham or sausage. After a meal we're more inclined to bring on the stinky and blue with dessert wine. Of course, if you're enjoying a rich, béchamel-laced mac-and-cheese casserole, we'd recommend skipping a cheese course altogether.

Here are our favorite accompaniments by cheese type.

Fresh

Think savory or sweet, depending on which fresh cheese you choose:

Goat (Petit Billy, Westfield Capri): hazelnut or walnut dressing, citrusy dressing, honey

Ricotta: fresh apricots; berries, including black-

berries, blueberries, and raspberries; fresh
figs; honey; rose water

Mozzarella: arugula, basil, figs (dried or fresh),
olive oil, tomato (fresh or sun-dried)

Bloomy

Think plump, juicy, or tangy to offset that thick,
buttery paste. We keep it simple: grapes, especially Muscat, and sourdough baguette.

Washed Rind

Think aromatic or spicy that can go head-to-head
with varying degrees of pungency: shavings of
fennel; fennel or pepper crackers; our favorite—
semolina raisin fennel bread from Amy's Bread,
next door to Murray's.

Semisoft

Think bold and tart with the combination of
creamy, moist paste and rustic, woodsy aromas:
walnut rye bread; acidic, concentrated fruitiness
of dried cherries and cranberries.

Firm

Think rustic and bold, depending on which firm
cheese you're eating:

Cheddar and Cheddar types: ale, apples, chutney,
cider (hard or not), pickled onions

*Sheep, aged (Manchego, Ossau-Iraty, Pecorino
Toscano):* apples, figs (dried or fresh),
Marcona almonds (Spanish almonds fried in
olive oil), *mostardes* (spicy fruit jellies), olives,
quince paste

*Mountain cheeses (Beaufort, Emmenthaler,
Gruyère):* Classic in a croque monsieur sandwich with bread, mustard, and ham; melt and

serve with boiled potatoes, gherkins, and crusty bread. The sweet, fruity flavors of the cheese are better with savory accompaniments.

Hard
Think savory and earthy, with luscious mouthfeel to offset the dry, caramelly inclination of these super-aged big guns: arugula, aged balsamic vinegar, fig jam, prosciutto.

Blue
Think sweet (to balance salt), earthy, and bitter/juicy: celery, chestnut honey, dates, endive, pears, port, walnuts, walnut raisin bread.

CHEESE Plates and PARTIES

Composing a cheese plate that will impress your friends (and yourself!) is relatively easy, if you follow these few guidelines:

1. Cheese should always be served at room temperature. Remove it from the fridge at least an hour before serving.
2. Cut the portions while the cheese is still cool.
3. Clean the knife between cuts so the flavors don't mix.
4. Arrange the cheeses on the plate from mildest to strongest, with the first cheese in the twelve o'clock position and the rest going clockwise.
5. Cover the pieces with parchment or wax paper to keep them from drying out.
6. Figure an ounce of each cheese per person, assuming a selection of three to five cheeses.
7. Using this number, a pound of cheese will take you quite far, comfortably serving fourteen to sixteen people.

The following lists cover the seven primary cheese types within this handbook; we've provided ten examples for each type.

- Pick five of the seven types (they're listed here from mildest to strongest, the order in which they should be plated).

- Pick one cheese from each type.

- Check out the guide for recommended beverage pairings and accompaniments.

- Enjoy!

Fresh

1. Banon
2. Burrata
3. Consider Bardwell Farm Mettowee
4. Crottin
5. Mozzarella di Bufala Campana
6. Petit Billy
7. Robiola di Roccaverano
8. Sainte-Maure-de-Touraine
9. Selles-sur-Cher
10. Valençay

Bloomy

1. Bittersweet Plantation Dairy Fleur-de-Lis
2. Brie de Meaux
3. Bucheron
4. Camembert de Normandie
5. Cremeux de Bourgogne (or other triple-crème)
6. Cypress Grove Humboldt Fog
7. Jasper Hill Constant Bliss
8. La Tur
9. Pérail
10. Saint-Marcellin

Washed Rind

1. Cato Corner Hooligan
2. Cowgirl Creamery Red Hawk
3. Durrus
4. Epoisses de Bourgogne
5. Langres
6. Pont-l'Evêque
7. Stinking Bishop
8. Taleggio
9. Tarentais
10. Vacherin Mont d'Or

Semisoft

1. Azeitao
2. Brin d'Amour
3. Charollais
4. Garrotxa (Queso de la Garrotxa)
5. Morbier
6. Pecorino Marzolino
7. Pecorino Tartufello
8. Saint-Nectaire
9. Ticklemore
10. Tomme Crayeuse

Firm

1. Cheddar, English Farmhouse
2. Comté
3. Gruyère, cave aged
4. Hoch Ybrig
5. Major Farm Vermont Shepherd
6. Manchego (Queso Manchego)
7. Pecorino Ginepro
8. Pecorino Toscano
9. Pyrénées Brebis
10. Uplands Cheese Company Pleasant Ridge Reserve (Extra Aged)

Hard

1. Berkswell
2. Coolea
3. Cypress Grove Midnight Moon
4. Gouda (preferably Boerenkaas)
5. Mahon
6. Mimolette
7. Parmigiano-Reggiano
8. Piave
9. Podda Classico
10. Vella Dry Jack

Blue

1. Bleu d'Auvergne
2. Cabrales (Queso Cabrales)
3. Cashel Blue
4. Fourme d'Ambert
5. Gorgonzola
6. Jasper Hill Bayley Hazen Blue
7. Persillé de Malzieu
8. Rogue Creamery Rogue River Blue
9. Roquefort
10. Stilton

TOP CHOICES FOR . . .

CHEESES BEFORE A MEAL

Our guiding principle before a meal: What will whet the appetite? For us, this tends to mean lighter cheeses, or something with a bit of salt to sharpen hunger, and cheeses that are happily at home beside savory noshes like prosciutto, salami, mixed olives, and nuts. Our favorites include:

Chevrot
Crottin de Chavignol
Manchego (aged or young)
Parmigiano-Reggiano
Pecorino Toscano (aged or young)
Petit Billy
Piave
Provolone, Mandarone

CHEESES WITH SALAD

Remember the first time you enjoyed crunchy ice-berg lettuce bathed in blue cheese dressing and gussied up with bacon? We do, too. One of the best showcases for cheese is as an essential ingredient in a hearty mixed salad. But the question is, What kind of salad?

The balance of textures and of bitter, salty, and acid flavors are important to consider. These are some of our favorite combinations, by salad type:

1. *Tender, buttery greens like Boston lettuce, mâche, and microgreens:* Crumbles or discs of fresh chèvre (goat cheese) such as Crottin, Crottin de Chavignol, Cypress Grove Humboldt Fog, Petit Billy, or Westfield Capri.

2. *Bitter or peppery greens, including arugula, frisée, and watercress:* Shavings of sweet and/or nutty cheese such as aged Gouda, Parmigiano-Reggiano, aged Pecorino Toscano, Piave, or Podda Classico.

3. *Bitter, slightly crunchy endive:* Thin shavings of the fruity, slightly sweet and nutty Swiss classics like Appenzeller, Gruyère, and Tête de Moine. Or go with a punchy, creamy blue like Roquefort.

4. *Rugged, grassy greens, including spinach and chard (best with some crisped bacon):* Crumbles of spicy blue cheese such as Cabrales, Gorgonzola (*piccante* or mountain), Maytag Blue, Point Reyes Farmstead Cheese Company Original Blue, or Roquefort. Or try a thick, creamy blue cheese dressing made by crumbling a fatty blue such as Bleu d'Auvergne,

Cashel Blue, Fourme d'Ambert, Gorgonzola (*cremificato*), or Rogue Creamery Oregon Blue Vein with a splash of cream.

5. *Fresh, juicy summer tomato:* Look for lactic, butterfatty fresh cheeses such as Burrata, Mozzarella, and Mozzarella di Bufala Campana.

CHEESES FOR GRILLED CHEESE SANDWICHES

Not all cheeses melt well, so experiment freely, and don't be afraid to use those odd cheese bits in your fridge. Grating often aids melting.

You can approach the ultimate grilled cheese sandwich in one of three ways:

Trendy, as in the current panini craze, where cheese and other ingredients are layered between ciabatta or other flatbread and pressed until gooey.

Simple, as in putting cheese on some type of bread, open-faced, under a broiler or toaster oven until the top is crusty brown and the middle is molten.

Classic, as in good white bread with minimal stuffing, smeared on the outside with copious amounts of butter and fried in a cast-iron pan.

Our favorites include these combinations:
1. Cheddar (classic, with bacon and tomato)
2. Fontina d'Aosta (trendy, with prosciutto and artichoke hearts)

3. Gruyère, cave aged (classic, with thinly sliced ham and whole-grain mustard)
4. Mozzarella, fresh or smoked (trendy, with sun-dried or fresh tomato and basil)
5. Provolone (simple, with crusty Italian bread and black olive paste)

MOST INTIMIDATING CHEESES

Think your friends are well-educated foodies? Think again . . .

1. Bleu de Termignon
2. Cabrales
3. Chiabro d'Henry
4. Evora
5. Pecorino di Fossa
6. Salers
7. Stanser Fladä
8. Stanser Schafchäs
9. Stinking Bishop
10. Tomme Vaudoise

SEXIEST CHEESES

No further introduction necessary.

1. Banon
2. Brillat-Savarin
3. Burrata/Mozzarella (warm from the vat)
4. Camembert de Normandie
5. Gorgonzola (Cremificato)
6. Jasper Hill Constant Bliss
7. Langres
8. La Serena (Queso de la Serena)
9. La Tur
10. Vacherin Mont d'Or

CHEESES TO EAT BEFORE YOU DIE

1. Boerenkaas (four-year)
2. Brie de Meaux and/or Camembert de Normandie
3. Burrata
4. Cheddar, English Farmhouse
5. Chevrotin
6. Major Farm Vermont Shepherd
7. Parmigiano-Reggiano (our producer of choice is Bonati)
8. Stilton (Colston Bassett)
9. Uplands Cheese Company Pleasant Ridge Reserve (Extra Aged)
10. Vacherin Mont d'Or

FAIL-SAFE CHEESE AND WINE PAIRINGS

1. Camembert de Normandie and Pinot Noir
2. Cheddar, English farmhouse, and Cabernet Sauvignon
3. Cowgirl Creamery Mt. Tam and Chardonnay
4. Ossau-Iraty-Brebis Pyrénées and Merlot
5. Parmigiano-Reggiano and Lambrusco
6. Robiola Bosina and Pinot Gris/Pinot Grigio
7. Roquefort and Sauternes
8. Selles-sur-Cher and Sauvignon Blanc
9. Stilton and Port
10. Triple-crème (Brillat-Savarin, Pierre-Robert) and Champagne

GLOSSARY

Alpage: A French term for the Alpine fields where animals graze in open air during the summer months. This rich, varied, seasonal diet contributes to milk (and cheese) that is considered superior for its depth, nuance, and complexity.

Amanteigado: Term used for the style of buttery, soft, raw sheep's-milk cheese typical of southern Spain and Portugal, which is coagulated using the cardoon thistle plant. These cheeses are often puddinglike, aged for thirty to forty-five days, and have an acidic, vegetal flavor.

Annatto: Extracted from the outer seed covering of the Central and South American "lipstick plant" *(Bixa orellana)*, otherwise known as the annatto tree, annatto is commonly added to cheese to create an orange-colored paste, as in **Mimolette**, and is presumed to have no effect on flavor. Also known as roucon.

Artisanal cheese: A small-production cheese handmade using traditional methods, though the cheesemaker may not own the milking animals directly.

Bloomy: A subcategory of soft-ripened cheese, with white, moldy, "blooming" rinds thanks to the addition of *Penicillium candidum*. Also known as "white rind." Aromas of wet straw and mushroom complement the buttery, melting paste. When ripe, these cheeses feel like the webbing between your fingers.

Brevibacterium linens (B. linens): The intentional bacteria cultivated on the surface of washed-rind cheeses, which create the orange or pinkish hue and the exceptional stink. *B. linens* requires a low-acid environment, moisture, and oxygen to flourish.

Cheddar: Technically, any cheese made by the method of "cheddaring," wherein curds are cut into small bits, cooked, and stacked into blocks. Generally, a cheese with a firm paste and noticeable acidity (sharpness). The best English farmhouse Cheddars are produced in Somerset, cloth bound, and made of raw cow's milk, though there is no protection on the name, and "Cheddar" can be made anywhere.

Cooked cheese: Cheese made by the process of heating and then holding (all the while stirring) a mixture of cheese curds and whey to a specific temperature to expel whey. Cooked-curd cheeses are typically aged, often for upwards of one year, and offer a firmer paste, toast and brown butter aromas, and sweet, sharp, nutty flavors. Classics include **Swiss Gruyère** and **Parmigiano-Reggiano**. In our guide, these fall into the firm and hard types of cheese.

Creamline: That luscious, oozing creaminess between the rind and the paste of a bloomy, washed-rind, or semi-soft cheese. The mold or bacterial activity on the rind breaks down (literally digests) the solid paste into a liquid.

Double-crème: A cream-enriched cheese (usually soft and bloomy) with at least 60 percent butterfat. Luscious, mild, and sweet in flavor.

Farmstead/farmhouse/*fermier* cheese: Small-production cheese made following traditional methods using the milk of animals raised on the cheesemaking premises.

Geotrichum candidum: A yeastlike mold used secondarily in the maturation of bloomy and washed-rind cheeses. In the former, it grows prior to the development of a bloomy rind and prevents the *P. candidum* from overtaking a cheese and leading to bitterness. In washed-rind cheeses, it is used to deacidify the surface of the cheese, creating a hospitable environment for the *B. linens*.

Goaty: A cheesehead's term for pronounced animal aromas and flavors in cheeses made from goat's milk, especially younger, softer varieties. The taste can come across as aggressively tangy.

Homogenization: The process of emulsifying the fat in milk to create a uniform texture and prevent separation of the cream. Milk is forced through a very fine membrane, pulverizing the fat into tiny bits that remain suspended. This is why the cream no longer rises to the top of your milk.

Paste or pâte: Term for the "meat" of a cheese, that edible part beneath the outer rind. The paste can range in texture from loose, soft, and buttery to firm and smooth to hard, dry, and crunchy.

Pasteurization: The heat treatment of milk with the intention of destroying potentially harmful microorganisms. Pasteurization is required of all cheeses produced in, or imported to, the United States that are less than sixty days old.

Penicillium candidum (P. candidum): A variant of the mold *P. camemberti*, which is a typical white, bloomy mold that becomes grayish after several days. The *P. candidum* variant remains white and is the trademark of a bloomy cheese. This surface mold, given the proper salt and moisture, will develop a rind that breaks down amino acid chains from the outside in, creating over time an increasingly soft, buttery texture.

Penicillium glaucum (P. glaucum): The lesser-known strain of blue mold used in some (typically milder) blue cheeses, such as **Gorgonzola**. See *Penicillium roqueforti*.

Penicillium roqueforti (P. roqueforti): The blue-green mold typical of blue cheeses, responsible for the breakdown of fats and the resulting piquant flavors. In addition, this mold deacidifies the cheese curds, which softens the texture over time.

Pressed cheese: Any cheese that is pressed after coagulation, cutting, and cooking (if applicable), draining of whey, and shaping of curds. Semisoft, firm, and hard cheeses are all pressed to achieve a smooth, uniform paste, while most bloomy and blue cheeses are not pressed at all—hence their lighter, moister texture.

Raw milk: Milk that has not been pasteurized. See Pasteurization.

Rennet: One of four substances used to break down milk protein for coagulation during cheesemaking.

Animal rennet is an enzyme (chymosin or rennin) most commonly taken from the fourth stomach of an unweaned calf. Vegetable rennet is derived from artichoke, butterwort, thistle, or nettle, which may produce a bitter flavor. Microbial rennet, developed in the 1970s, uses an enzyme extracted from mold as its active ingredient and is suitable for vegetarians. FPC (fermented-produced chymosin) is a genetically modified product that claims no residual animal organisms and is also suitable for vegetarians.

Roucou: See Annatto.

Sheepy: A cheesehead's term for pronounced animal aromas and flavors in cheeses made of sheep's milk, such as lanolin or "gaminess" (as in lamb chops and wild game meats).

Tomme: A French term meaning "smallish round of cheese." Tommes are often identified by their region of origin, as in **Tomme de Savoie**. Small tommes are known as *tommettes*.

Transhumance: The traditional migration of animals from valley to mountain pastures during the spring and summer, following the melting snow and new grass.

Triple-crème: A cream-enriched cheese with a minimum fat content of 75 percent. Nearly all triple-crèmes are made in the bloomy style.

Ubriaco: Drunk, in Italian. A general term for the Italian style of wine-washed or grape must–encrusted cheeses traditionally made of cow's milk in northern Italy, but increasingly produced elsewhere.

Unpasteurized milk: Milk that has not been pasteurized. Synonymous with raw milk. See Pasteurization.

Vegetarian cheese: A cheese containing a nonanimal-derived coagulant. See Rennet.

Washed rind: A subcategory of soft-ripened cheese. Lower-acid curds are washed in brine (salt water), often containing beer, wine, or spirits to promote the growth of the bacterium *B. linens*. Soft to semisoft in texture, with a strong, pungent aroma and full, salty flavor.

BIBLIOGRAPHY

Baboin-Jaubert, Alix. *Handbook of Cheese*. London: Hachette Illustrated, 2003.

Boisard, Pierre. *Camembert: A National Myth*. Translated by Richard Miller. Berkeley: University of California Press, 2003.

Canut, Enric. *Los 100 Quesos Espanoles*. Barcelona: Salvat, 2000.

Fiori, Giacomo. *Formaggi Italiani*. Verolengo: EOS Editice, 1999.

Jenkins, Steven. *The Cheese Primer*. New York: Workman, 1996.

Kinstedt, Paul. *American Farmstead Cheese: The Complete Guide to Making and Selling Artisan Cheeses*. White River Junction, VT: Chelsea Green, 2005.

Masui, Kazuko, and Tomoko Yamada. *French Cheeses*. London: Dorling Kindersley, 1996.

Piumatti, Gigi, Roberto Rubino, and Piero Sardo, eds. *Italian Cheese: A Guide to Their Discovery and Appreciation*. Bra, Italy: Slow Food Arcigola Editore, 1999–2000.

Planck, Nina. *Real Food: What to Eat and Why*. New York: Bloomsbury, 2006.

Rance, Patrick. *The French Cheese Book*. London: Macmillan, 1989.

———. *The Great British Cheese Book*. London: Macmillan, 1982.

Studd, Will. *Chalk and Cheese*. Melbourne Purple Egg, 1999.

Tewksbury, Henry. *The Cheeses of Vermont*. Woodstock, VT: Countryman Press, 2002.

INDEXES

Vacherin Fribourgeois
Vacherin Mont d'Or
Vella Dry Jack
Vento d'Estate
Weinkase

Goat's Milk
Banon
Bittersweet Plantation Dairy
  Evangeline
Bucheron
Cabra Penamacor
Capra Valtellina
Caprino Noce
Capriole Farm O'Banon
Chabichou du Poitou
Charollais
Chèvre Noir
Chevrot
Chevrotin
Chiabro d'Henry
Cone du Port Aubry
Consider Bardwell Farm
  Mettowee
Crottin
Crottin de Chavignol
Cypress Grove Humboldt
  Fog
Cypress Grove Midnight
  Moon
Drunken Goat (Queso de
  Murcia al Vino)
El Suspiro (Torta de los
  Montes de Toledo)
Feta, French
Garrotxa (Queso de la
  Garrotxa)
Goat Gouda
Harbourne Blue
Ibores (Queso de los
  Ibores)
Innes
Juniper Grove Tumalo
  Tomme
Kasseri
Lazy Lady La Petite Tomme
Le Sarlet
Le Valleroger
Lively Run Cayuga Blue
Maconnais
Manouri
Maxidome Chèvre
Monte Enebro (Queso del
  Tietar)

Mozzarella Company Hoja
  Santa
Nettle Meadow Kunik
Nevat
Ossera Serrat Gros (Queso
  de Ossera)
Pélardon
Persillé de Chèvre du
  Beaujolais
Petit Billy
Pouligny-Saint-Pierre
Ribafria
River's Edge Tillamook Burn
Sainte-Maure-de-Touraine
Sally Jackson Cheeses
Selles-sur-Cher
Suau de Cluau (Queso del
  Montsec)
Tarentais
Ticklemore
Tomme de la Chataigneraie
Tomme de l'Ariège
Tomme des Templiers
Valençay
Vare (Queso Vare)
Westfield Capri
Westfield Classic Blue Log

Mixed Milk
Amarelo da Beira Baixa
Cabrales (Queso Cabrales)
Cravanzina
Gabietou
Gamonedo (Queso
  Gamonedo)
Gjetost
Grazalema (Queso de
  Grazalema)
Halloumi
Kasseri
La Tur
Manouri
Old Chatham Camembert
Peaked Mountain Ewe
  Jersey
Peral (Queso de Peral)
Podda Classico
Robiola Bosina
Robiola di Roccaverano
Robiola Rossa
Robiola Vite
Saint Hannois
Toledo
Tomme du Berger

Tommette des Alpes
Tommette Morgée au
   Seyssel
Valdéon (Queso Picon
   Bejes-Treviso)

Sheep's Milk
Ardi-Gasna
Azeitao
Beenleigh Blue
Bellwether Farm San
   Andreas
Berkswell
Brin d'Amour
Crozier Blue
Erborinato di Pecora
Evora
Feta, Bulgarian
Feta, French
Feta, Greek
Fiore Sardo
Fleur du Maquis
Idiazábal (Queso Idiazábal)
Kasseri
La Serena (Queso de la
   Serena)
Lavort
Lord of the Hundreds
Lovetree Trade Lake Cedar
Major Farm Vermont Shepherd
Manchego (Queso
   Manchego)
Manouri
Old Chatham Shepherd's
   Wheel
Ossau-Iraty-Brebis Pyrénées
Pata de Mulo (Queso Pata
   de Mulo)
Pecorino Crotonese
Pecorino di Fossa
Pecorino di Pienza
Pecorino Foglie de Noce
Pecorino Ginepro
Pecorino Imperatore
Pecorino Marzolino
Pecorino Nero di Siena
Pecorino Oro Antico
Pecorino Pepato
Pecorino Romano
Pecorino Tartufello
Pecorino Toscano
Pérail
Persillé de Malzieu
Pyrénées Brebis

Ricotta
Ricotta Salata
Roncal (Queso Roncal)
Roquefort
Saint Blaise
Sally Jackson Cheeses
Serpa
Serra da Estrela
Stanser Schafchäs
Tommette de Lucciana
Torta del Casar (Queso Torta
   del Casar)
Vento d'Estate
Willow Hill Summer Tomme
Zamorano (Queso
   Zamorano)

Abondance
Affidelice
Aisy Cendré
Ardi-Gasna
Banon
Beaufort d'Alpage
Bethmale
Bleu d'Auvergne
Bleu de Termignon
Bleu du Haut-Jura (Bleu de
   Gex)
Brie
Brie de Meaux
Brie de Melun
Brie de Nangis
Brillat-Savarin
Brin d'Amour
Bucheron
Camembert de Normandie
Chabichou du Poitou
Chaource
Charollais
Chevrot
Chevrotin
Comté
Cone du Port Aubry
Cremeux de Bourgogne
Crottin
Crottin de Chavignol
Délice de Bourgogne
Délice de Saint-Cyr
Epoisses de Bourgogne
Feta, French
Fleur du Maquis
Fougerus
Fourme d'Ambert
Fromage d'Affinois
Fromage de Meaux
Gabietou
Gaperon
Laguiole
L'Ami du Chambertin
Langres
Lavort
L'Edel de Cleron
Le Sarlet
Le Valleroger
Livarot
Maconnais
Maroilles
Maxidome Chèvre
Mimolette
Morbier
Munster/Munster-Géromé

Ossau-Iraty-Brebis Pyrénées
Pavé d'Auge
Pélardon
Pérail
Persillé de Chèvre du
   Beaujolais
Persillé de Malzieu
Persillé du Beaujolais
Petit Billy
Pierre-Robert
Pont-l'Evêque
Pouligny-Saint-Pierre
Pyrénées Brebis
Raclette
Reblochon
Rigotte
Rocbleu
Roquefort
Saint Blaise
Sainte-Maure-de-Touraine
Saint-Félicien
Saint Hannois
Saint-Marcellin
Saint-Nectaire
Saint-Paulin
Salers
Sechons de l'Isere
Selles-sur-Cher
Soumaintrain
Tarentais
Tomme Crayeuse
Tomme de la Chataigneraie
Tomme de l'Ariège
Tomme de Loubière
Tomme de Savoie
Tomme des Templiers
Tomme du Berger
Tommette de Lucciana
Tommette des Alpes
Tommette Morgée au
   Seyssel
Valençay

Greece
Feta, Greek
Kasseri
Manouri

Holland
Cypress Grove Midnight
   Moon
Goat Gouda
Gouda

Mahon
Manchego (Queso Manchego)
Monte Enebro (Queso del Tietar)
Nevat
Ossera Serrat Gros (Queso de Ossera)
Pata de Mulo (Queso Pata de Mulo)
Peral (Queso de Peral)
Roncal (Queso Roncal)
Serrat del Triado
Suau de Cluau (Queso del Montsec)
Tetilla (Queso de Tetilla)
Torta del Casar (Queso Torta del Casar)
Valdeón (Queso Picon Bejes-Treviso)
Vare (Queso Vare)
Zamorano (Queso Zamorano)

Switzerland
Alpage Prattigau
Appenzeller
Emmenthaler
Försterkäse
Gruyère
Hoch Ybrig
Raclette
Stanser Fladä
Stanser Röteli
Stanser Schafchäs
Tête de Moine
Tomme Vaudoise
Vacherin Fribourgeois
Vacherin Mont d'Or
Weinkase

USA
Antigo Cheese Company Stravecchio
Bellwether Farm Carmody (Reserve)
Bellwether Farm San Andreas
Bittersweet Plantation Dairy Evangeline
Bittersweet Plantation Dairy Fleur-de-Lis
Capriole Farm O'Banon

Cato Corner Bridgid's Abbey
Cato Corner Drunken Hooligan
Cato Corner Drunk Monk
Cato Corner Hooligan
Cobb Hill Ascutney Mountain
Cobb Hill Four Corners Caerphilly
Consider Bardwell Farm Mettowee
Cowgirl Creamery Mt. Tam
Cowgirl Creamery Red Hawk
Crave Brothers Les Freres
Cypress Grove Humboldt Fog
Fiscalini Bandaged Cheddar
Fiscalini San Joaquin Gold
Grafton Four Star Cheddar
Great Hill Blue
Jasper Hill Aspenhurst
Jasper Hill Bartlett Blue
Jasper Hill Bayley Hazen Blue
Jasper Hill Constant Bliss
Jasper Hill Winnimere
Juniper Grove Tumalo Tomme
Lazy Lady La Petite Tomme
Limburger
Lively Run Cayuga Blue
Lovetree Trade Lake Cedar
Major Farm Vermont Shepherd
Maytag Blue
Meadow Creek Grayson
Morning Fresh Dairy Blue
Mozzarella Company Hoja Santa
Nettle Meadow Kunik
Oakvale Farmhouse Gouda
Old Chatham Camembert
Old Chatham Shepherd's Wheel
Peaked Mountain Ewe Jersey
Point Reyes Farmstead Cheese Company Original Blue, Monty's Reserve
River's Edge Tillamook Burn

Rogue Creamery Oregon
   Blue Vein
Rogue Creamery Rogue
   River Blue
Rogue Creamery Smokey
   Blue
Roth Käse Sole Gran Queso
Sally Jackson Cheeses
Sonoma Cheese Factory
   Sonoma Jack
Sprout Creek Toussaint
Taylor Farm Smoked Gouda
Teleme
Thistle Hill Tarentaise
Uplands Cheese Company
   Pleasant Ridge Reserve
   (Extra Aged)
Vella Dry Jack
Westfield Capri
Westfield Classic Blue Log
Willow Hill Summer Tomme

Wales
Caerphilly
Llangloffan
Saval

BY PASTEURIZATION
Raw
Abbaye de Cîteaux
Abondance
Alpage Prattigau
Amarelo da Beira Baixa
Appenzeller
Ardi-Gasna
Asiago d'Allevo
Azeitão
Banon
Beaufort d'Alpage
Bellwether Farm San
   Andreas
Berkswell
Bitto
Bleu de Termignon
Bleu du Haut-Jura (Bleu de
   Gex)
Brescianella Stagionata
Brie de Meaux
Brie de Melun
Cabrales (Queso Cabrales)
Cabra Penamacor
Camembert de Normandie
Caprino Noce

Castelmagno
Cato Corner Bridgid's
   Abbey
Cato Corner Drunken
   Hooligan
Cato Corner Drunk Monk
Cato Corner Hooligan
Chabichou du Poitou
Charollais
Cheddar, Keen's
Cheddar, Montgomery's
Chevrotin
Chiabro d'Henry
Cobb Hill Ascutney
   Mountain
Cobb Hill Four Corners
   Caerphilly
Comté
Cone du Port Aubry
Crottin de Chavignol
Délice de Saint-Cyr
Durrus
Emmenthaler
Erborinato di Pecora
Evora
Fiscalini Bandaged Cheddar
Fiscalini San Joaquin Gold
Fontina d'Aosta
Försterkäse
Gabietou
Gamonedo (Queso
   Gamonedo)
Grafton Four Star Cheddar
Grana Padano
Great Hill Blue
Gruyère
Hoch Ybrig
Ibores (Queso de los
   Ibores)
Idiazábal (Queso Idiazábal)
Innes
Jasper Hill Aspenhurst
Jasper Hill Bartlett
Blue
Jasper Hill Bayley Hazen
   Blue
Jasper Hill Constant Bliss
Jasper Hill Winnimere
Juniper Grove Tumalo
   Tomme
Laguiole
L'Ami du Chambertin
La Serena (Queso de la
   Serena)

Lavort
Le Valleroger
Lincolnshire Poacher
Lively Run Cayuga Blue
Llangloffan
Lord of the Hundreds
Lovetree Trade Lake Cedar
Major Farm Vermont
  Shepherd
Maconnais
Maroilles
Maytag Blue
Meadow Creek Grayson
Montasio
Oakvale Farmhouse Gouda
Ossau-Iraty-Brebis
  Pyrénées
Ossera Serrat Gros (Queso
  de Ossera)
Parmigiano-Reggiano
Pata de Mulo (Queso Pata
  de Mulo)
Pavé d'Auge
Peaked Mountain Ewe
  Jersey
Pecorino di Fossa
Pecorino Ginepro
Pecorino Marzolino
Pecorino Nero di Siena
Pecorino Tartufello
Pélardon
Pérail
Persillé de Chèvre du
  Beaujolais
Persillé de Malzieu
Persillé du Beaujolais
Point Reyes Farmstead
  Cheese Company
  Original Blue, Monty's
  Reserve
Pouligny-Saint-Pierre
Provolone, Mandarone
Pyrénées Brebis
Reblochon
Rigotte
Robiola di Roccaverano
Robiola Rossa
Robiola Vite
Rogue Creamery Oregon
  Blue Vein
Rogue Creamery Rogue
  River Blue
Rogue Creamery Smokey
  Blue

Roncal (Queso Roncal)
Roquefort
Saint Blaise
Sainte-Maure-de-Touraine
Saint Hannois
Salers
Sally Jackson Cheeses
Saval
Sechons de l'Isere
Selles-sur-Cher
Serpa
Serra da Estrela
Serrat del Triado
Sprout Creek Toussaint
Stanser Fladä
Stanser Röteli
Stanser Schafchäs
Tarentais
Taylor Farm Smoked
  Gouda
Tête de Moine
Thistle Hill Tarentaise
Tomme Crayeuse
Tomme de la Chataigneraie
Tomme de l'Ariège
Tomme de Loubière
Tomme des Templiers
Tomme du Berger
Tommette de Lucciana
Tommette des Alpes
Tommette Morgée au
  Seyssel
Tomme Vaudoise
Torta del Casar (Queso Torta
  del Casar)
Uplands Cheese Company
  Pleasant Ridge Reserve
  (Extra Aged)
Valençay
Vella Dry Jack
Weinkase
Zamorano (Queso
  Zamorano)

Pasteurized
Antigo Cheese Company
  Stravecchio
Ardrahan
Arzúa Ulloa (Queso de
  Arzúa-Ulloa)
Asiago Pressato
Basket Cheese
Beenleigh Blue
Bishop Kennedy

Vare (Queso Vare)
Vento d'Estate
Westfield Capri
Westfield Classic Blue Log
Willow Hill Summer Tomme

Raw/Pasteurized
Affidelice
Afuega'l Pitu
Aisy Cendré
Bellwether Farm Carmody
  (Reserve)
Bethmale
Bleu d'Auvergne
Bra Tenero or Duro
Brie
Brillat-Savarin
Brin d'Amour
Caciocavallo Silano
Caerphilly
Chaource
Cheddar, Quicke's
Cheshire
Chimay
Crottin
Double Gloucester
Epoisses de Bourgogne
Fiore Sardo
Fleur du Maquis
Fougerus
Fourme d'Ambert
Gaperon
Gouda
Grazalema (Queso de
  Grazalema)
Lancashire
Langres
Livarot
Mahon
Manchego (Queso
  Manchego)
Morbier
Munster/Munster-Géromé
Oka
Pecorino di Pienza
Pecorino Foglie de Noce
Pecorino Pepato
Pecorino Toscano
Pont-l'Evêque
Raclette
Raschera
Saint-Félicien
Saint-Marcellin
Saint-Nectaire

Saint-Paulin
Soumaintrain
Tomme de Savoie
Ubriaco al Prosecco
Ubriaco Gran Riserva
Vacherin Fribourgeois
Vacherin Mont d'Or

BY TYPE
Fresh
Banon
Basket Cheese
Burrata
Caprino Noce
Capriole Farm O'Banon
Cone du Port Aubry
Consider Bardwell Farm
  Mettowee
Crottin
Crottin de Chavignol
Feta, Bulgarian
Feta, French
Feta, Greek
Halloumi
Innes
Maconnais
Mozzarella
Mozzarella Company Hoja
  Santa
Mozzarella di Bufala
  Campana
Petit Billy
Ricotta
Rigotte
River's Edge Tillamook
  Burn
Robiola
Robiola di Roccaverano
Robiola Vite
Sainte-Maure-de-Touraine
Selles-sur-Cher
Valençay
Westfield Capri
Westfield Classic Blue Log

Bloomy
Bittersweet Plantation Dairy
  Evangeline
Bittersweet Plantation Dairy
  Fleur-de-Lis
Brie
Brie de Meaux
Brie de Melun

Brie de Nangis
Brillat-Savarin
Bucheron
Camembert de Normandie
Chaource
Cowgirl Creamery Mt. Tam
Cravanzina
Cremeux de Bourgogne
Cypress Grove Humboldt
    Fog
Délice de Bourgogne
Délice de Saint-Cyr
Fougerus
Fromage d'Affinois
Fromage de Meaux
Jasper Hill Constant Bliss
La Tur
Lazy Lady La Petite Tomme
L'Edel de Cleron
Le Sarlet
Maxidome Chèvre
Nettle Meadow Kunik
Nevat
Old Chatham Camembert
Old Chatham Shepherd's
    Wheel
Paglietta
Pélardon
Pérail
Pierre-Robert
Robiola Bosina
Robiola Rossa
Saint-Félicien
Saint-Marcellin
Stracchino
Tomme Vaudoise

Durrus
Epoisses de Bourgogne
Fontina d'Aosta
Försterkäse
Gubbeen
Jasper Hill Farm Winnimere
L'Ami du Chambertin
Langres
Le Valleroger
Limburger
Livarot
Maroilles
Meadow Creek Grayson
Milleens
Munster/Munster-Géromé
Oka
Pavé d'Auge
Pont-l'Evêque
Raclette
Reblochon
Saint Blaise
Saint-Paulin
Saval
Slack Ma Girdle
Soumaintrain
Stanser Fladä
Stanser Röteli
Stanser Schafchäs
Stinking Bishop
Taleggio
Tarentais
Tomme de l'Ariège
Tomme du Berger
Tommette Morgée au
    Seyssel
Vacherin Mont d'Or

Washed Rind

Abbaye de Cîteaux
Affidelice
Aisy Cendré
Ardrahan
Bishop Kennedy
Brescianella Stagionata
Cabra Penamacor
Cato Corner Drunken
    Hooligan
Cato Corner Drunk Monk
Cato Corner Hooligan
Chevrotin
Chimay
Cowgirl Creamery Red
    Hawk
Crave Brothers Les Freres

Semisoft

Afuega'l Pitu
Amarelo da Beira Baixa
Arzúa Ulloa (Queso de
    Arzúa-Ulloa)
Asiago Pressato
Azeitão
Bethmale
Bra Tenero or Duro
Brin d'Amour
Caerphilly
Castelmagno
Castelrosso
Cato Corner Bridgid's
    Abbey
Chabichou du Poitou
Charollais

Chevrot

Drunken Goat (Queso de Murcia al Vino)

El Suspiro (Torta de los Montes de Toledo)

Fleur du Maquis

Gaperon

Garrotxa (Queso de la Garrotxa)

Juniper Grove Tumalo Tomme

Kasseri

La Serena (Queso de la Serena)

Lovetree Trade Lake Cedar

Monte Enebro (Queso del Tietar)

Morbier

Oakvale Farmhouse Gouda

Ossera Serrat Gros (Queso de Ossera)

Pecorino di Fossa

Pecorino Marzolino

Pecorino Nero di Siena

Pecorino Tartufello

Pecorino Toscano

Pouligny-Saint-Pierre

Raschera

Ricotta Salata

Saint Hannois

Saint-Nectaire

Sally Jackson Cheeses

Salva Cremasco

Scamorza

Serpa

Serra da Estrela

Sharpham Rustic

Sonoma Cheese Factory Sonoma Jack

Sottocenere

Suau de Cluau (Queso del Montsec)

Taylor Farm Smoked Gouda

Teleme

Tetilla (Queso de Tetilla)

Ticklemore

Tomme Crayeuse

Tomme de la Chataigneraie

Tomme de Loubière

Tomme de Savoie

Tomme des Templiers

Tommette de Lucciana

Tommette des Alpes

Torta del Casar (Queso Torta del Casar)

Vacherin Fribourgeois

Weinkase

Firm

Abondance

Alpage Prattigau

Appenzeller

Ardi-Gasna

Beaufort d'Alpage

Bellwether Farm Carmody (Reserve)

Bellwether Farm San Andreas

Bitto

Bra Tenero or Duro

Caciocavallo Silano

Capra Valtellina

Cheddar, Keen's

Cheddar, Montgomery's

Cheddar, Quicke's

Cheshire

Chèvre Noir

Chiabro d'Henry

Cobb Hill Four Corners Caerphilly

Comté

Double Gloucester

Emmenthaler

Evora

Fiore Sardo

Fiscalini Bandaged Cheddar

Fiscalini San Joaquin Gold

Gabietou

Grafton Four Star Cheddar

Grazalema (Queso de Grazalema)

Gruyère

Hoch Ybrig

Ibores (Queso de los Ibores)

Idiazábal (Queso Idiazábal)

Jasper Hill Aspenhurst

Laguiole

Lancashire

Lavort

Lincolnshire Poacher

Llangloffan

Lord of the Hundreds

Major Farm Vermont Shepherd

Manchego (Queso Manchego)

Manouri
Montasio
Ossau-Iraty-Brebis Pyrénées
Pata de Mulo (Queso Pata
de Mulo)
Peaked Mountain Ewe
Jersey
Pecorino Crotonese
Pecorino di Pienza
Pecorino Foglie de Noce
Pecorino Ginepro
Pecorino Imperatore
Pecorino Oro Antico
Pecorino Pepato
Pecorino Romano
Pecorino Toscano
Provolone, Auricchio
Pyrénées Brebis
Ribafria
Roncal (Queso Roncal)
Roth Käse Sole Gran Queso
Salers
Sechons de l'Isere
Sprout Creek Toussaint
Tête de Moine
Thistle Hill Tarentaise
Toledo
Ubriaco al Prosecco
Ubriaco Gran Riserva
Uplands Cheese Company
Pleasant Ridge Reserve
(Extra Aged)
Vare (Queso Vare)
Vento d'Estate
Zamorano (Queso
Zamorano)

Hard
Antigo Cheese Company
Stravecchio
Asiago d'Allevo
Berkswell
Cobb Hill Ascutney Mountain
Coolea
Cypress Grove Midnight
Moon
Gjetost
Goat Gouda
Gouda
Grana Padano
Laguiole
Lancashire
Mahon
Mimolette

Parmigiano-Reggiano
Piave
Podda Classico
Provolone, Mandarone
Serrat del Triado
Vella Dry Jack

Blue
Beenleigh Blue
Bleu d'Auvergne
Bleu de Termignon
Bleu du Haut-Jura (Bleu de
Gex)
Cabrales (Queso Cabrales)
Cashel Blue
Crozier Blue
Erborinato di Pecora
Fourme d'Ambert
Gamonedo (Queso
Gamonedo)
Gorgonzola
Great Hill Blue
Harbourne Blue
Jasper Hill Bartlett Blue
Jasper Hill Bayley Hazen
Blue
Kapiti Kikorangi
Lively Run Cayuga Blue
Maytag Blue
Peral (Queso de Peral)
Persillé de Chèvre du
Beaujolais
Persillé de Malzieu
Persillé du Beaujolais
Point Reyes Farmstead
Cheese Company Original
Blue, Monty's Reserve
Rocbleu
Rogue Creamery Oregon
Blue Vein
Rogue Creamery Rogue
River Blue
Rogue Creamery Smokey
Blue
Roquefort
Shropshire Blue
Stilton
Valdeón (Queso Picon
Bejes-Treviso)

VEGETARIAN CHEESES
Antigo Cheese Company
Stravecchio

Azeitão
Beenleigh Blue
Bellwether Farm Carmody
  (Reserve)
Berkswell
Bittersweet Plantation Dairy
  Evangeline
Bittersweet Plantation Dairy
  Fleur-de-Lis
Cashel Blue
Cobb Hill Ascutney
  Mountain
Cobb Hill Four Corners
  Caerphilly
Consider Bardwell Farm
  Mettowee
Cowgirl Creamery Mt. Tam
Cowgirl Creamery Red
  Hawk
Crozier Blue
Cypress Grove Humboldt
  Fog
Evora
Fiscalini Bandaged Cheddar
Fiscalini San Joaquin Gold
Grafton Four Star Cheddar
Gubbeen
Harbourne Blue
Innes
Kapiti Kikorangi
La Serena (Queso de la
  Serena)
Lively Run Cayuga Blue
Lord of the Hundreds
Lovetree Trade Lake Cedar
Mozzarella Company Hoja
  Santa
Old Chatham Camembert
Old Chatham Shepherd's
  Wheel
Point Reyes Farmstead
  Cheese Company
  Original Blue, Monty's
  Reserve
River's Edge Tillamook Burn
Rogue Creamery Oregon
  Blue Vein
Rogue Creamery Rogue
  River Blue
Rogue Creamery Smokey
  Blue
Roth Käse Sole Gran Queso
Saval

Serpa
Serra da Estrela
Sharpham Rustic
Shropshire Blue
Slack Ma Girdle
Sprout Creek Toussaint
Stilton (in all cases except
  Colston Bassett)
Stinking Bishop
Ticklemore
Torta del Casar (Queso Torta
  del Casar)
Vella Dry Jack
Westfield Capri
Westfield Classic Blue Log
Willow Hill Summer Tomme

NAME-PROTECTED
  CHEESES
A.O.C.
Abondance
Banon
Beaufort d'Alpage
Bleu d'Auvergne
Bleu du Haut-Jura (Bleu de
  Gex)
Brie de Meaux
Brie de Melun
Camembert de Normandie
Chabichou du Poitou
Chaource
Chevrotin
Comté
Crottin de Chavignol
Epoisses de Bourgogne
Laguiole
Langres
Livarot
Maroilles
Munster/Munster-Géromé
Ossau-Iraty-Brebis
  Pyrénées
Pont-l'Evêque
Pouligny-Saint-Pierre
Reblochon
Roquefort
Sainte-Maure-de-Touraine
Saint-Nectaire
Salers
Selles-sur-Cher
Vacherin Mont d'Or
Valençay

D.O.
Arzúa Ulloa (Queso de
Arzúa-Ulloa)
Cabrales (Queso Cabrales)
Drunken Goat (Queso de
Murcia al Vino)
Gamonedo (Queso
Gamonedo)
Ibores (Queso de los
Ibores)
Idiazábal (Queso Idiazábal)
La Serena (Queso de la
Serena)
Mahon
Manchego (Queso
Manchego)
Roncal (Queso Roncal)
Tetilla (Queso de Tetilla)
Torta del Casar (Queso Torta
del Casar)
Zamorano (Queso
Zamorano)

D.O.P. (Italy)
Asiago d'Allevo
Asiago Pressato
Bitto
Bra Tenero or Duro
Caciocavallo Silano
Castelmagno
Fiore Sardo
Fontina d'Aosta
Gorgonzola
Grana Padano
Montasio
Mozzarella di Bufala
Campana
Parmigiano-Reggiano
Pecorino Toscano
Raschera
Robiola di Roccaverano
Taleggio

D.O.P. (Portugal)
Amarelo da Beira Baixa
Azeitão
Evora
Serpa
Serra da Estrela

Barbera
Caprino Noce
Castelrosso

Beaujolais (Gamay grape)
Abbaye de Cîteaux
Chèvre Noir
Fromage d'Affinois
Gabietou
Major Farm Vermont
Shepherd
Peaked Mountain Ewe
Jersey
Pérail
Persillé du Beaujolais
Tomme du Berger

Bordeaux (Cabernet Sauvignon, Merlot, Cabernet Franc, Petit Verdot, and Malbec grapes)
Bethmale
Reblochon
Saint-Nectaire
Serra da Estrela

Burgundy (Pinot Noir grape)
Bleu de Termignon
Brie de Melun
Camembert de Normandie
Cremeux de Bourgogne
L'Ami du Chambertin
Llangloffan
Major Farm Vermont
Shepherd
Tommette de Lucciana

Cabernet Sauvignon
Cheddar, Montgomery's
Cypress Grove Midnight
Moon
Epoisses de Bourgogne
Fiscalini Bandaged Cheddar
Kapiti Kikorangi
Lincolnshire Poacher
Pecorino Crotonese
Podda Classico
Roth Käse Sole Gran Queso

Saint-Paulin
Vella Dry Jack

Cahors (Merlot and Malbec grapes)
Uplands Cheese Company
    Pleasant Ridge Reserve
    (Extra Aged)

Carmignano
Pecorino Imperatore
Scamorza

Côtes du Rhône (Syrah, Grenache, Mourvèdre, and other grapes)
Brie de Meaux
Brie de Nangis
Comté
Fleur du Maquis
Fromage de Meaux
Gruyère
Laguiole
Morbier
Saint-Félicien
Saint-Marcellin
Tomme de Savoie
Torta del Casar (Queso Torta
    del Casar)

Dolcetto
Bra Tenero or Duro

Douro (Tinta Roriz, Touriga Nacional, Tinta Nacional, and Tinta Barroca grapes)
Azeitão

Malbec
Ardi-Gasna
Berkswell
Mimolette

Merlot
Brie
Cato Corner Bridgid's
    Abbey
Cheddar, Quicke's
Gaperon
Hoch Ybrig
Mahon
Pata de Mulo (Queso Pata
    de Mulo)

Pecorino Romano
Piave
Raclette
Teleme

Montepulciano
Pecorino Pepato

Nebbiolo (as in Barbaresco and Barolo)
Bra Tenero or Duro
Castelmagno
Chiabro d'Henry
Fontina d'Aosta
Lancashire
Lord of the Hundreds
Pecorino Ginepro
Podda Classico
Robiola Rossa
Ubriaco Gran Riserva

Pinot Noir (Oregon)
Beaufort d'Alpage
Bellwether Farm San
    Andreas
Crave Brothers Les Freres
Juniper Grove Tumalo
    Tomme
Pecorino Ginepro
Podda Classico
River's Edge Tillamook Burn
Rogue Creamery Oregon
    Blue Vein
Rogue Creamery Smokey
    Blue
Sally Jackson Cheeses

Ribera del Duero (Tempranillo, Garnacha, and other grapes)
Idiazábal (Queso Idiazábal)
Zamorano (Queso
    Zamorano)

Rioja (Tempranillo, Garnacha, and other grapes)
Afuega'l Pitu
Drunken Goat (Queso de
    Murcia al Vino)
Idiazábal (Queso Idiazábal)
Manchego (Queso
    Manchego)
Pecorino Oro Antico

Roncal (Queso Roncal)
Serra da Estrela
Serrat del Triado
Toledo

Rosé
Banon
Feta, French
Kasseri
Saint Blaise

Sangiovese (as in Chianti and Chianti Classico)
Caciocavallo Silano
Fiore Sardo
Lord of the Hundreds
Montasio
Pecorino di Fossa
Pecorino Nero di Siena
Pecorino Oro Antico
Pecorino Tartufello
Pecorino Toscano
Provolone, Auricchio
Provolone, Mandarone

Syrah/Shiraz
Abondance
Bethmale
Bleu d'Auvergne
Coolea
Goat Gouda
Gouda
Peral (Queso de Peral)
Pyrénées Brebis
Salers
Sprout Creek Toussaint
Tomme Crayeuse

Valpolicella (Corvina, Molinara, and Rondinella grapes)
Bitto
Cato Corner Drunken Hooligan
Lincolnshire Poacher
Pecorino Foglie de Noce

Zinfandel
Antigo Cheese Company Stravecchio
Coolea
Emmenthaler
Gjetost

Goat Gouda
Gouda
Provolone, Mandarone

WHITE WINE

Albariño
Amarelo da Beira Baixa
Arzúa Ulloa (Queso de Arzúa-Ulloa)
Chevrot
Garrotxa (Queso de la Garrotxa)
Nevat
Tetilla (Queso de Tetilla)
Vare (Queso Vare)

Arneis
Raschera
Robiola Vite

Bordeaux (Sauvignon Blanc, Sémillon, and Muscadelle grapes)
Fougerus
Old Chatham Camembert

Chardonnay (Burgundy)
Affidelice
Aisy Cendré
Charollais
Cowgirl Creamery Mt. Tam
Délice de Bourgogne
Lovetree Trade Lake Cedar
Maconnais
Peaked Mountain Ewe Jersey
Pérail
Rigotte
Sechons de l'Isere
Tomme des Templiers

Chardonnay (California)
Bellwether Farm Carmody (Reserve)
Brie
Grazalema (Queso de Grazalema)
Mahon
Oakvale Farmhouse Gouda
Sonoma Cheese Factory Sonoma Jack
Vacherin Fribourgeois
Weinkase

Chenin Blanc
Bittersweet Plantation Dairy
    Evangeline
Durrus
Gubbeen
Harbourne Blue
Lazy Lady La Petite Tomme
Maxidome Chèvre
Milleens
Stanser Fladä
Tarentais
Westfield Classic Blue Log

Côtes du Rhône (Clairette, Grenache Blanc, Ugni Blanc, Roussanne,Viognier, and other grapes)
Försterkäse
Saint Hannois
Ticklemore
Tomme du Berger

Fumé Blanc (Sauvignon Blanc)
Brin d'Amour
Cowgirl Creamery Red
    Hawk
Ricotta Salata
Rocbleu
Willow Hill Summer Tomme

Gavi (Cortese grape)
Robiola di Roccaverano

Gewürztraminer
Appenzeller
Great Hill Blue
Jasper Hill Winnimere
Munster/Munster-Géromé
Pavé d'Auge
Tommette Morgée au
    Seyssel
Vacherin Mont d'Or

Grüner Veltliner
Délice de Saint-Cyr

Muscat
Bleu du Haut-Jura (Bleu de
    Gex)
Erborinato di Pecora
Monte Enebro (Queso del
    Tietar)

Orvieto (Trebbiano, Malvasia, and Grechetto grapes)
Asiago d'Allevo
Capra Valtellina
Pecorino Marzolino

Pinot Blanc
Stanser Schafäs
Tomme de Loubière
Vento d'Estate

Pinot Grigio/Pinot Gris
Asiago Pressato
Brescianella Stagionata
Halloumi
Robiola Bosina
Salva Cremasco
Taleggio
Tommette des Alpes

Retsina
Feta, Greek

Riesling
Chevrotin
Cypress Grove Humboldt
    Fog
Durrus
Emmenthaler
Epoisses de Bourgogne
Lively Run Cayuga Blue
Old Chatham Shepherd's
    Wheel
Pélardon
Soumaintrain
Tomme de l'Ariège

Rioja (Malvasia, Garnacha Blanca, and Viura grapes)
El Suspiro (Torta de los
    Montes de Toledo)
Ibores (Queso de los
    Ibores)
Suau de Cluau (Queso del
    Montsec)

Sauvignon Blanc
Brin d'Amour
Bucheron
Chabichou du Poitou
Chevrot
Cone du Port Aubry